Pg 21, 22, 27, 45
→ Pg 96 (t)

D1617258

Annexing Mexico

Solving the Border Problem through Annexation and Assimilation

By Erik Rush

Level 4 Press, Inc.

Dedication

I would like to dedicate this book to all those Americans working on numerous fronts who today, in the face of derision, calumny and various forms of excoriation, strive to keep in focus the vision of the Founding Fathers of the United States of America.

Acknowledgements

I would like to thank William Roetzheim, the Publisher of Level 4 Press, Inc., for his recognition of the problems contained herein and his interest, infectious excitement and support during the process. In addition, I would like to acknowledge the dozens of people and organizations who provided the anecdotal and statistical information necessary to transform this concept from mere hopeful mental musings or an opinionated rant into the viable protocol I believe it is now.

Once again, I would like to thank my family, friends, readers and supporters who help to keep me on track, reminding me why I'm doing what I'm doing, and how important it is to our country.

Published by
Level 4 Press, Inc.
13518 Jamul Drive
Jamul, CA 91935
www.level4press.com

BISAC Subject Heading: SOC007000   SOCIAL SCIENCE / Emigration & Immigration
Library of Congress Control Number: 2006937614

ISBN: 978-1-933769-23-3

Printed in China

Preface

For it is never to be forgotten that self-defense is the first law of nature and of nations. If that man who careth not for his own household is worse than an infidel, the nation which permits its institutions to be endangered by any cause which can fairly be removed, is guilty not less in Christian than in natural law. Charity begins at home; and while the people of the United States have gladly offered an asylum to millions upon millions of the distressed and unfortunate of other lands and climes, they have no right to carry their hospitality one step beyond the line where American institutions, the American rate of wages, the

> *American standard of living, are brought into serious peril.*
> *Francis A. Walker in The Atlantic Monthly, 1896[i]*

These words are as true today as they were when they were spoken in 1896. Our problems would all go away if we just followed the arguments of Patrick Buchanan to their logical conclusion and deported all of the illegal aliens, along with the descendants of those illegal aliens.

Hey, wait a second. If my great grandfather was an illegal immigrant from Germany, jumping ship in New York to flee economic depression in Germany for better financial opportunities in the United States, that would mean I'd have to go back to Germany!

No, here's what I meant to say: "*We* belong here, but *they* must go!" Everyone agrees with this on some level, and always has. In fact, it's true throughout all of human history. The only thing that changes is the definition of "we" and the definition of "they."

If "we" are the European whites and "they" are the minorities, then it won't be long before "we" are in the minority and, in a democracy, we might very well become a "they."

If "we" are the European whites, blacks and a select few other groups who've been here awhile, and "they" are those of Mexican descent, it might not be long before "we" are in the minority as well. "We" again become a "they."

Is that a frightening prospect?

Given the fact that I happen to be of mixed race (including German), for the record I'm obviously venturing into the realm of the theoretical.

Maybe Marcos Guitiérrez was not too far off when he said:

> *"The Mexican-US connection cannot be stopped. Politicians should know that we are here to stay and at one point in history we will be in power. How you treat us now, will determine how we'll treat you once the roles are reversed."[ii]*

In 2005, I wrote two columns addressing the U.S.-Mexico border crisis. *The Case for Annexing Mexico* was presented as an almost tongue-in-cheek proposition, primarily because I believed that even my regular readers and the like-minded were going to think it was somewhat over the top, possessing some reasonable concepts and talking points—but something that was as likely to be seriously considered by America as a mass emigration of Americans to Haiti.

The impetus for writing the piece was the release in August 2005 of a published survey of Mexicans by the Pew Hispanic Center, which indicated that more than 40 percent of Mexican adults would emigrate to the United States if they could.

Annexing Mexico Revisited was a bit more sober, and that's because of the astounding amount of feedback I received in favor of the idea following the first column. Granted, many who thought favorably of the first column didn't think the idea would ever catch on, but just as many even provided reasonably practical ideas and policies toward implementing the annexation. I found it noteworthy that this constructive criticism came from people who identified themselves as independents, liberals, conservatives; some even claimed not to have much interest in political machinations at all.

The most critical opposition came after release of the first column; this was from the Mexican *La Crónica de Hoy,* which painted me as one of those intolerant, conservative Christian oppressors, right up there with broadcaster and one-time presidential candidate Pat Robertson. This was around the same time Robertson, of the

Christian Broadcasting Network, suggested that it might behoove the Bush administration to have U.S. intelligence operatives assassinate Venezuela's Marxist leader Hugo Chavez.

The United States has been compared to the Roman Empire at the height of its power. Perhaps we should remember that the Roman empire collapsed not from a planned, concerted barbarian assault but from an overwhelming influx of nomadic Huns and various Germanic tribes that eventually overwhelmed the capacity of their civilization to assimilate them. Yet the United States is attempting to assimilate 36 million foreigners in a generation, with 1.5 million more from various third world nations added to the number each year. Unfortunately, as long as immigrants (legal and illegal) from Mexico are lumped together with other immigrants to North America, the problem will never be solved. The United States may not be able to solve all the world's problems, but we most assuredly have the resources to solve many of the problems on this continent. All that we're lacking is the necessary vision.

This book is divided into the following sections:

A Border Crisis describes the current, extremely bleak situation. I hope that everyone reading this chapter will be left angry that the Federal government has allowed the situation to deteriorate to where it is today, and determined to do something about it.

How the United States Became the United States provides a history of US expansionism since our inception, with a particular emphasis on expansionism vis-à-vis Mexico.

The Rights of Man reinforces the idea that governments exist to serve the population, not vice versa, and looks at the "score card" of the US government versus the Mexican government in terms of this philosophy.

We All Win addresses the benefits both to the United States and to Mexico of incorporating Mexico into the United States.

Send in the Marines discusses how this might be accomplished.

Who Pays the Bill addresses the costs of integration and looks at potential sources of funds.

Let's Get Some Balls wraps things up with a challenge to move forward.

Appendix A is a chronology of relevant events.

Appendix B describes the Border Patrol's Secure Border Initiative in their own words.

Appendix C is the official history of the INS from their own documents.

Appendix D contains the official statements as to how the Customs and Immigration service has secured the border from the threat of nuclear smuggling.

Appendix E is a copy of the full text of the Mexican Government released comic book that offers advice to illegal immigrants.

Appendix F is a report from the FAIR website on Immigration's Impact on the US.

Appendix G is a set of talking points related to the "FAIR Tax" proposal for a replacement to the income tax system, something that is mentioned very briefly in the body of the book.

Appendix H is a list of reference books, and Appendix I contains the endnotes.

A Border Crisis

*Give me your tired, your poor,
Your huddled masses,
yearning to breathe free,
The wretched refuse
of your teeming shore.
Send these, the homeless,
tempest-tost to me:
I lift my lamp beside the
golden door.*
Emma Lazarus
poem at the Statue of Liberty

&&&

"...we do have the ultimate weapon. People are more mobile now. They can go anywhere. In a borderless world we can go anywhere. If we are not allowed a good life in our countries, if we are going to be global citizens, then we should migrate North. We should migrate North in our millions, legally or otherwise. ...if there is any strength that we

> *have, it is in numbers. Three-fourths of the world is either black, brown, yellow, or some combination of all these. ...This is how we will ultimately challenge globalization...if we are not allowed a piece of the action, a piece of the cake; if we are not allowed to prosper in a border-less world."*
> Dr. Data Seri Mahathir bin Mohamad[iii]

I recall once seeing news footage of food being distributed to starving refugees by aid workers. Unfortunately, there was not enough food to feed everyone and the starving throngs stampeded the truck filled with food, killing or injuring both themselves and the aid workers and spilling much of the food.

In some sense, the United States can be thought of as that relief truck, doing our best to help the Third World but getting torn apart and trampled in the process.

We're going to cover a lot of ground in this chapter. If you think you're saving money paying less per hour for your gardener, you're going to be shocked to learn how much money was tickled out of your wallet while you leaned over to give him his sandwich and iced tea. Now, I'm no more suggesting every Mexican gardener without a green card is a kleptomaniac than I am suggesting black people have tails, but that 1) people who commit illegal acts (like unlawfully entering someone's country) generally have a proclivity toward such acts, and 2) statistics unequivocally bear out that we have essentially imported a veritable Pandora's box of nefarious enter- prises and criminality through our pitiful border policies. This is to say nothing rela- tive to the *unseen costs* of illegal immigra- tion, which follows presently.

Then there are the immigrants crossing our borders with turbans on their heads and satchel bombs on their backs, more interested in mowing down our population than our yards. I will address this aspect of our deficiency in this area, the reasons for it, and the manifest insanity of subscribing to "politically-correct" notions of dealing with same.

Finally, I'll present the ultimate, workable solution to this problem for those who are open-minded, on the fence, or whiners who maintain that the border is too long to ef- fectively seal off.

But first, let's see how bad things really are. After all, if this whole immigration thing is as complicated as the "experts" say it is, perhaps we should just ignore it— leave its disposition to politicians, statesman and captains of industry who "know what they're doing."

Yeah. *Right...*

Immigration is Out of Control

"The most obvious threat is the fact that...there are going to be 120 million Mexicans [in the U.S.] by the end of the century... [The Border Patrol] will not have enough bullets to stop them."

William Colby
Former CIA Director

Estimates of the number of illegal immigrants in the United States vary between ten and thirty million, with government estimates tending toward the low end; estimates by business tending toward the middle; and estimates by xenophobes tending to the high end. More significant than the absolute number is the rate of increase. The number of illegal aliens flooding into the US this *year* will total 3 million[iv]—enough to fill 22,000 Boeing 737-700 aircraft with attendees to the largest *fiesta* any nation has ever thrown. Add another 1.3 million legal immigrants to this and you'll start to get an indication of the magnitude of the problem. In fact, immigration accounted for nearly 80% of the US population growth in the last decade and. If you include children of immigrants (who are automatically U.S. citizens upon birth), we're pretty much up to 100% of the population growth. Contrast this with average job growth between 1999 and 2005 (of 1.226 million jobs[v]) and you'll notice that we've got more people arriving than we have new jobs created. So what about our kids who are entering the workforce hoping for employment? Sorry, we've already got plenty of applicants and they're willing to work for minimum wage!

Many frequently respond along the lines of, "but we've always been a nation of immigrants." Fair enough. It's not the concept that is creating problems, but the magnitude and the implementation, which has been subverted by greed and the insinuation of perverse political philosophies.

In his book *A Nation of Immigrants* John F. Kennedy said:

> *"The gates were now flung open, and men and women in search of a new life came to these shores in ever-increasing numbers—150,000 in the 1820s, 1.7 million in the 1840s, 2.8 million in the 1870s, 5.2 million in the*

1880s, 8.8 million in the first decade of the 20th century...

Between 1830 and 1930, the period of the greatest migration from Europe to the United States, Germany sent six million people to the United States—more than any other nation...

Italy has contributed more immigrants to the United States than any other country except Germany. Over five million Italians came to this country between 1820 and 1963.vi"

During the 350 years from 1607 to 1963 when President Kennedy wrote these words, a total of 42 million immigrants came to the United States. Today, our foreign-born population is greater than the entire 42 million immigrants that arrived during that 300-year period. The Border Patrol apprehends as many illegal immigrants *every month* as the entire number of legal immigrants in 1820. Just take a moment to absorb that fact: There are more *illegal* immigrants in the US today than all of the Italian and German immigrants (that Kennedy cited) combined. In fact, more people emigrate to the US (legally and illegally) than emigrate to all of the rest of the countries in the world combined.

The East County region of San Diego is a case in point. Thirty years ago ranchers put out water cups by wells to quench the thirst of the occasional traveler hiking from Mexico into the US. Sure, they were illegal but they were just ordinary folks. Then the fences started to get cut, the dogs poisoned, the trash left in huge piles, the bands of armed men carrying drugs, etc. Now that rancher goes around armed and locks his doors at night in fear — or more often, leaves.

The legal and illegal immigrant count is only part of the statistical total. U.S. law says that with few exceptions (primarily concerning foreign diplomats here on official duty) a child born in this country is eligible for U.S. citizenship whether not its parents are here legally. Mexican mothers frequently come to the United States just to give birth, taking advantage of free, state-of-the-art medical care in hospital emergency rooms, guaranteed U.S. citizenship for her child and eligibility for a wide range of social services programs that are automatically available to the new U.S. citizen. Ambulances from Mexico routinely bring patients, including expectant mothers, to US hospital emergency rooms.

There's no need for them to sneak across the border—border agents simply wave them across the border. One Customs official explained, "We are not medical people. We don't have that kind of expertise. We don't know. Somebody says they are sick, we wave them on in."[vii] One-tenth of all children born in the United States, and 22% of children born in California[viii], are "anchor babies", and in accordance with the federal Emergency Medical Treatment & Labor Act (EMTALA) any doctor or hospital that refuses to treat these "emergency" cases is subject to a $50,000 fine[ix].

It gets even better. Once you've got an infant U.S. citizen, the mother and father are eligible to emigrate to take care of the child. And hey, you can't leave behind those brothers and sisters. And grandma. And grandpa. The list keeps growing, starting with the anchor baby and continuing through what's termed "chain migration."

Now, before you develop a major resentment around those young Mexican mothers, ask yourself this question: "If you were a young Mexican mother wouldn't you do the same thing?" I, as well as many conservatives and many of my colleagues, don't blame them; we blame our Congress for allowing our policies to mutate into a system where this kind of thing is not only possible, it's positively condoned. To the

8

best of my knowledge, we are the only country in the world that works this way. As one talk radio personality recently quipped: "You try to sneak into *other* countries, and they shoot you."

Just in case you are among those who still harbor the naïve thought that Mexico might help to stem the tide from their end, think again: Why would they want to? The number two source of foreign currency in Mexico is remittances sent home by Mexican workers in the U.S. That's right: Mexico gets more money from illegal émigrés to the United States than it gets from tourism or foreign direct investment (it's second only to money generated in *maquiladoras*, or border factories).[x] In fact, the Mexican Foreign Ministry published a thirty-two page comic book titled *The Guide for the Mexican Immigrant* that included tips such as[xi]:

- If you cross by desert, try to walk at times when the heat will not be too intense.

- If you get lost, guide yourself by light posts, train tracks, or dirt roads.

- If you decide to hire people traffickers to cross the border, consider the following precautions:
- Do not let them out of your sight. Remember that they are the only ones who know the lay of the land, and therefore the only ones who can get you out of that place.
- It is better to be arrested for a few hours and repatriated to Mexico than to get lost in the desert.

- Avoid noisy parties. The neighbors can get annoyed and call the police, and you can be arrested.

The fact is that the Mexican government has every reason to encourage and support migration of laborers (legal and illegal) to the United States and, to date, no reason whatsoever to discourage same.

What's become painfully evident to residents living close to the border (on *both* sides) is another unfortunate aspect of the wave of illegal immigration: Many of those folks walking through the desert and hills aren't coming here to cut grass—they're here to sell grass (and cocaine, and crystal meth, and heroin, and so on). Now, I happen to think the Mexican government has a point when it blames the U.S. for the drug problem. We're the ones buying the stuff. We're the ones who made it illegal and thereby created a hugely profitable, violent underground network. We're the ones who allowed our society to degrade morally and culturally to the point where there's a market for illicit drugs in the first place.

The point here however, is that drugs are integrated into this cross-border smuggling effort and the end result is violence. Incursions by armed Mexican paramilitary and military units have become increasingly common. Our government has documented 231 incursions from 1996 to 2005 involving Mexican military, state, or municipal police units. And it's getting worse. *Much* worse. The book *In Mortal Danger* describes one such incursion:[xii]

> On January 23, 2006, three SUVs were seen fording the Rio Grande at Neely's Crossing. Hudspeth County, Texas, sheriff's deputies gave chase, and the SUVs turned back and

11

headed toward the river. There the caravan was met by a military-style Humvee with a mounted .50-caliber machine gun on the U.S. side of the river. One SUV blew a tire short of the river and was abandoned by the smugglers. One made it back across the river, but the third got stuck. A dozen men in battle-dress uniforms with AK-47 rifles appeared on the Mexican side of the river and helped to unload many bales of contraband from the marooned SUV. The sheriff's deputies and highway patrol officers could only watch because they were outgunned and outmanned. After unloading their cargo, the Mexicans set fire to the SUV, leaving it to burn in the riverbed.

Not to worry; our Bureau of Customs and Border Protection has solved the problem by issuing Border Patrol agents a wallet card containing the following advice (among other things):

Remember: Mexican Army personnel are trained to evade, es-

cape, and counter-ambush if necessary to escape.

Maybe Caspar Weinberger, President Reagan's Secretary of Defense, wasn't so far off in his book *The Next War* when he described a wartime scenario with Mexico in which the U.S. tries unsuccessfully to defend the border using 60,000 U.S. troops[xiii].

The apathetic, the ignorant, and those in the business community who are dependent on cheap labor are of the mindset: *Hey, let 'em come.* In fact, the latter group lobbies like crazy to make this possible. You've heard the phrase "Short-term sacrifice for long-term gain"? Well, this is "short-term profit (theirs) for long-term pain (ours)"; their collective political power negates that of many a politician's constituency.

We've all heard journalists and elected officials propose "cracking down on companies who hire illegals"—but how do you think this plays with politicians who have such companies among their constituents, in their counties or states, who will see tax revenues plummet when this "crackdown" goes down? How does it play with the congressman, congresswoman or senator who has such companies in their district or state, companies that assure them they'll be shot from a cannon next election if they're pressured to stop hiring illegals? *Think,* people...

The steady supply of labor willing to work for below market wages and without benefits certainly keeps payroll costs down, but let's look at the true, overall cost of this approach to our society.

Can You Say "Staggering"?

A 1997 study estimated that the total net cost to the Federal Government for legal and illegal immigrants was $70 billion annually.[xiv] This number is the net of services used by immigrants balanced against taxes paid in. Over 62% of the net national cost of immigration in 1996, $40.6 billion, was attributable to legal and legalized (those who received amnesty) immigrants. Illegal immigration generates about 38%, $24 billion of the total net cost.

Of course, the rate of immigration since 1997 has soared, so the costs have increased. Dr. Donald Huddle estimates the 2006 net annual costs at $108 billion.[xv]

Then there are the State costs. A 1996 study[xvi] estimated these costs at:

- California: $28 billion
- New York: $14 billion
- Texas: $7 billion

- Florida: $6 billion

Based on immigration rates, these numbers would be roughly doubled today. In fact, the lifetime net fiscal drain for adult immigrants is $55,200[xvii], although the largest cost of all could actually be depressed wages and job loss for our own children, a cost estimated at $133 billion annually.[xviii]

The financial picture tells only part of the story, of course. There are other costs that are more difficult to quantify. Things such as reduced quality and increased costs for healthcare, environmental problems, increased crime, and the influx of diseases endemic to other countries are but a few "quality of life" issues. Let's look at some of the more painful costs of immigration in detail.

Educational Costs

> *"The level of immigration is so massive, it's choking the urban schools. It's bad enough when you have desperate kids with U.S. backgrounds—we require massive resources. In come kids with totally different needs, and*

> *it creates crushing burdens on urban schools."*
>
> David W. Steward[xix]

As shown in the following table, the total cost to educate *illegal* immigrants and their U.S.-born children is estimated at $29 billion dollars[xx] with the top honors going to California ($8 billion); Texas ($4 billion); New York ($3 billion); and Illinois ($2 billion). To make matters worse, bringing a student with limited or no English skills up to an acceptable level requires an additional $10,000 per student. This is just with regard to the illegal immigrants. Over the past twenty years *all* of the growth in the school-age population has been the result of children from legal and illegal immigrants. In 2005, there were 10.3 million school-age children from immigrant families in the United States.[xxi]

State	Illegal Immigrants		Their US Born Children		Total	
California	$	3,220	$	4,508	$	7,728
Texas	$	1,645	$	2,304	$	3,949
New York	$	1,306	$	1,829	$	3,135
Illinois	$	834	$	1,168	$	2,002
New Jersey	$	620	$	868	$	1,488
Florida	$	518	$	725	$	1,243
Georgia	$	397	$	555	$	952
North Carolina	$	321	$	450	$	771
Arizona	$	312	$	437	$	749
Colorado	$	235	$	329	$	564
Washington	$	229	$	321	$	550
Massachusetts	$	206	$	289	$	495
Virginia	$	189	$	264	$	453
Oregon	$	167	$	234	$	401
Michigan	$	135	$	190	$	325
Nevada	$	134	$	187	$	321
maryland	$	117	$	164	$	281
Minnesota	$	115	$	161	$	276
Pennsylvania	$	100	$	140	$	240
Connecticut	$	95	$	133	$	228
Indiana	$	86	$	120	$	206
Wisconsin	$	84	$	118	$	202
Kansas	$	80	$	112	$	192
Utah	$	77	$	108	$	185
Ohio	$	76	$	107	$	183
Oklahoma	$	67	$	94	$	161
Tennessee	$	65	$	91	$	156
New Mexico	$	64	$	89	$	153
South Carolina	$	60	$	84	$	144
Nebraska	$	43	$	61	$	104
Iowa	$	41	$	58	$	99
Arkansas	$	37	$	52	$	89
Missouri	$	37	$	52	$	89
Rhode Island	$	36	$	51	$	87
Alabama	$	34	$	48	$	82
Idaho	$	27	$	38	$	65
Delaware	$	22	$	31	$	53
Kentucky	$	22	$	30	$	52
DC	$	20	$	27	$	47
Other States	$	43	$	61	$	104
TOTAL	$	11,916	$	16,688	$	28,604

For years we've been hearing about the declining quality of education in California. Teachers have been blamed. Administrators have been blamed. Funding has been blamed. In short, everything has been blamed except the real problem—immigration. We hear a lot about falling test scores nationwide. According to the Educational Testing Service, native-born Americans scored 8 points above the average score of native-born citizens of the other sixteen nations that were measured, while U.S. immigrants scored 16 points below the average of immigrants in the other sixteen nations.[xxii] This phenomenon is obviously exacerbated in the state with the highest number of immigrants: California. With educators struggling to deal with non-English speaking, poorly educated, poorly performing immigrants in our schools, who suffers? *Our* children.

Many schools have given up on trying to teach traditional American curricula, opting instead for multi-cultural education taught in languages other than English. For all I know, if the kids close their eyes, they might not be aware they're in the United States at all. Think I'm kidding? In September 2005, a senior at Larkin High School in Elgin, Illinois was reprimanded and sent to the principal's office because he remained seated during the playing of the Mexican national anthem at a ceremony honoring Mexican Independence day.xxiii The people of Columbus, New Mexico got so fed up with their schools educating students from Palomas, Mexico for free that they sued. Julieta Avina, the Mayor of Palomas, responded, "The people behind the lawsuit must have come from someplace else. If they don't like Mexico they ought to move to Canada."xxiv

Well, Julieta, there's another option: We could move the United States down to Mexico—but first, let's look at another area of impact... Crime.

The Cost of Crime

> *"The border remains a military zone. We remain a hunted people. Now you think you have a destiny to fulfill in the land that historically has been ours for forty thousand years. And we're a new Mestizo nation. And they want us to discuss civil rights. Civil rights. What law made by white men to oppress all of us of color, female and male. This is our homeland. We cannot—we will not—and we must not be made illegal in our own home-*

19

land. We are not immigrants that came from another country to another country. We are migrants, free to travel the length and breadth of the Americas because we belong here. We are millions. We just have to survive. We have an aging white America. They are not making babies. They are dying. It's a matter of time. The explosion is in our population."
—José Angel Gutiérrez, Professor, University of Texas at Arlington, founder La Raza Unida Party at UC Riverside 1/1995

With diatribe like that coming from "educators" right here in the U.S., it's no wonder criminal elements from across the border are taking advantage of its porosity—and our government's faintness of heart. Despite the chilling belligerence and racism contained in the above quote, I've always been impressed with the level of character in the majority of Mexican immigrants I've encountered. Nice people, the sort of people I'd welcome as neighbors. This is, as they say, hardly the point.

I thought it was just bad luck when the wife of a California colleague was hit by a car full of drunk illegal aliens who fled the scene of the accident. At least, I thought that until it happened three times. In fact, I've since discovered that California leads the nation in hit and run accidents, including those involving fatalities.

This rather bothersome problem isn't limited to traffic violations, either. In fact, 95 percent of the outstanding homicide warrants and two-thirds of all felony warrants in Los Angeles are issued for illegal aliens, a total of more than *17,000 outstanding warrants*. In *one* city. Twelve thousand members of the 20,000 member strong "18th Street Gang" are illegal aliens.[xxv] More than 57,000 cars are stolen annually by illegal aliens in Phoenix, Arizona alone.[xxvi]

And is it any wonder? President George W. Bush has conceded that of the 4.5 million aliens caught attempting to break into the United States there were more than 350,000 with criminal records.[xxvii] That's 70,000 felons per year "escaping" into our backyard. Our police do the best that they can once these

criminals arrive, but between their traditional duties and the fact that many work
in "sanctuary" cities whose liberal city governments actually prohibit them from effectively detecting illegals, their hands are
quite often tied—or should I say cuffed?

Criminal aliens account for over 29 percent of prisoners in Federal Bureau of
Prison facilities[xxviii] and roughly an equal
percentage of the population of county jail
inmates in Los Angeles. Los Angeles alone
pays over $150 million dollars per year to
house inmates that should never have
been here in the first place. In all, the
United States spent $5.8 billion incarcerat-
ing illegal aliens in the three year period
between 2002 and 2005.[xxix] Note that this
is in addition to the more than $12 billion
spent on direct border enforcement in 2006
alone.[xxx]

Now, the average, law-abiding American
might surmise that once these criminals
served their time (at taxpayer expense) they
would be shipped back to their country of
origin with all due haste. In fact, more than
80,000 of these felons were simply returned to the streets once their prison sentence was done[xxxi], and we now find that
forty-five percent of them are usually re-
arrested after their release.[xxxii]

I guess that in one sense (the "we're a
nation of immigrants" sense, that is), this

is fair. A goodly number of the initial settlers in the U.S. were here under court order, because it was cheaper to exile them to the North American continent than to jail them in England. Now the rest of the world is doing it to us, in a perverse sort of "what goes around, comes around," right? Wrong. No one is "doing this to us"—we're doing it to ourselves!

So what's the solution? Move to a gated community with private security guards? Not unless they've created gates that are impermeable to germs...

Healthcare Costs

For the past 70 years, the research and medical community in the United States worked to eradicate many diseases, primarily through improved sanitation, vaccination, and testing. A great deal of this work was a success; everyone with school age children knows the drill of digging up vaccination records prior to their child starting school. Those in my generation remember mandatory tuberculosis tests for health care workers and teachers. I remember my father telling me of the kids in his grade school classes whom polio picked off when he was a boy. Some even died.

Well, all of that work finally paid off and diseases such as tuberculosis, polio, most intestinal parasites, and leprosy were virtually wiped out. Even many nuisance problems such as lice and bedbugs were virtually gone. Mosquitoes were virtually extinct throughout the U.S. OK—that's a lie. Just wanted to make sure you were paying attention. Wishful thinking, perhaps...

So what happened? Just as that proverbial (but historically notable) complacency set in, we find people coming here from countries that never did develop things like vaccinations or concepts of sanitation bringing those diseases and more with them. Let's start with a typical example: Tuberculosis.

I had the opportunity to be involved in tuberculosis research for several years at a major Western university. Tuberculosis is caused by the bacterium *Mycobacterium tuberculosis,* which most commonly affects the lungs; long-term infections have the potential to affect the central nervous system, lymphatic system, circulatory system, genitourinary system, bones and joints.

Tuberculosis is a Level 3 pathogen (the dreaded ebola is a Level 4 pathogen). Tuberculosis is transmitted person-to-person via aerosol; that is, much in the same way one catches a cold. *Granuloma* within the lungs (cystic formations resulting from the body "walling off" clusters of bacteria) eventually transform the lungs into calcified, useless scar tissue. Imagine having only one lung. Then imagine having half a lung; finally, imagine having only a golf ball-sized piece of lung viable enough to facilitate respiration—yet still being alive. It's a slow, painful process that rivals some of the worst cancers. Symptoms include chest pain, bloody sputum (coughed up blood), fever, chills, night sweats, appetite loss, weight loss, and fatigue. An individual can languish in this state for many years. Current chemotherapeutic regimens take months and are known for high liver toxicity.

The incidence of TB is one hundred times as high among immigrant children as among native-born children. Prince William County in Virginia saw a 188 percent increase in the TB rate, with 92 percent of all cases among the foreign born.[xxxiii] California recently reported *38,291* cases of tuberculosis.[xxxiv] Worse, frequent and incorrect usage of antibiotics throughout much of the Third World bred super-strains of the germ that are multiple drug resistant, with a 60 percent fatality rate and treatment cost of between $200,000 and $1,200,000 per patient. In fact, over the past five years illegal aliens from Mexico have brought 16,000 cases of multi-drug resistant (MDR) tuberculosis cases into the

US.xxxv MDR TB, by the way, is much more difficult to treat than non-MDR TB; it's even more of an ordeal. Hence the high price tag.

So, these TB bacteria readily fly through the air when a person coughs, potentially infecting anyone in the vicinity. Just to be clear, I'm talking about people like your children at school, you and your wife at the movies—in short, everyone. Studies have been done that one's chances of contracting TB while aboard commercial aircraft are exponentially higher if an infected individual happens to be aboard.

What other presents are illegal immigrants bringing to the U.S.?

• Leprosy was virtually unknown in the U.S. Suddenly, over the past three years we've got more than seven thousand reported cases and the disease is endemic to the Northeastern states;

• Malaria was obliterated in the US, but is now making a come-back in Texas;

• Polio (the crippling killer virus of the last century) was eradicated but is now making a comeback;

• Chagas, a tropical parasitic disease once unheard-of in North America but infecting eighteen million people and killing 50,000 annually south of the border is now found throughout the U.S. and is becoming a major threat to our blood supply. I'll wager you haven't heard about *this* one on the network news...

• Lice and bedbugs have both made comebacks throughout the U.S. Lice have proven to be a particular problem because the immigrant parents keep sending their children back to school without getting rid of the lice, thereby reinfecting their classmates.

In total, immigrants account for 65 percent of all communicable disease in the U.S., although they represent a significantly smaller percentage of the population. How much do you want to bet that of the 35 percent of U.S. natives infected with communicable disease, a significant percentage caught it from an immigrant?

In addition to the slight inconvenience you'll experience when your friendly gardener infects you with MDR TB, there is the hard financial cost to us as a nation. Emergency room medical treatment to illegal immigrants costs U.S. taxpayers over $1.4 billion. Since federal reimbursements don't begin to cover the true costs of the emergency room services, these emergency rooms and hospitals, are going bankrupt and shutting their doors. In California alone, eighty-four emergency rooms have closed, and those that remain open have waits of several hours due to crowds of illegal immigrants waiting their turn for free medical care. Providing free medical care to the uninsured has driven up the cost of medical insurance for everyone else to the point where one dollar of every five dollars spent in the United States will go toward health care. [xxxvi]

If you aren't yet convinced we have a *huge* problem by now, there can only be one of two reasons: You're either a liberal or a money-worshipping businessperson with no ethics or sense of civic responsibility whatsoever.

No, I understand, I really do. Your heart goes out to all of those poor, disease-ridden people from around the world. So does mine, believe it or not. Mother Teresa wouldn't turn them away just because they have leprosy or TB, right?

If you happen to be a liberal, you probably have a certain amount of concern for the environment too, correct? Having a sustainable planet and all that? Let's focus on the environment for a moment, shall we?

Environmental Costs

Those of us from the "Baby Boomer" generation remember the term Zero Population Growth, or ZPG. This was probably the most fundamental concept of "save our planet" movements in the 1970s. In 1972, the landmark Rockefeller Commission looked at the U.S. population of roughly 200 million and recommended:

> *After two years of concentrated effort, we have concluded that, in the long run, no substantial benefits will result from the further growth of the Nation's population—rather that a gradual stabilization of our population would contribute significantly to the Nation's ability to solve its problems.*[xxxvii]

Even Richard Nixon, not particularly known for being a rabid environmentalist, recognized the problem as early as 1969:

"In 1917 the total number of Americans passed 100 million, after three full centuries of steady growth. In

1967—just half a century later—the 200 million mark was passed. If the present rate of growth continues, the third hundred million persons will be added in roughly a thirty-year period. This means that by the year 2000, or shortly thereafter, there will be more than 300 million Americans. The growth will produce serious challenges for our society. I believe that many of our present social problems may be related to the fact that we have had only fifty years in which to accommodate the second hundred million Americans."

More recently, Gaylord Nelson, the father of the first Earth Day in 1970, said:

"All nations are degrading and consuming their environment to a point beyond capacity. In the past 15 years [1978-1993] in the U.S., we have added 1300 cities with populations over

100,000. When the environment is forced to file Chapter 11, the ecology collapses. Nations recover from war but not from a failed eco-system. The status of our environment is more threatening than all wars. It is forever."xxxviii

Native-born, environmentally conscious Americans listened to these dire warnings, jumped on the ZPG bandwagon, and adopted a slightly below replacement level of fertility since 1972. Based on this, the United States that we pass on to our children should have a population of slightly below 200 million, and falling. But wait, the US population isn't 200 million—in fact, during the week of October 16, 2006, it broke 300 million. What happened?

The federal government sabotaged us, that's what. By allowing massive immigration we've continued on the same population growth curve that everyone warned us about in 1970. The only difference between the dire predictions of environmentalists and leaders then and the reality today is that it's *other people's* children causing us to grow by 3 million people per year, not mine or yours.

The situation is even worse in our border states. In 1965, California had a population of 18 million. Today the state has 35 million and in another 25 years is expected to hit 55 million. California must build a new elementary school every day, 365 days per year, just to keep up with the increasing number of immigrant children. Many people think that California has grown because of people moving there from other parts of the country. This is fallacious.

For example, during the 1990s, immigrants and their children accounted for 100 percent of the population growth in California—a statistic that also holds true for New York, New Jersey, Illinois, and Massachusetts.

In 2001 "Mr. Earth Day," Gaylord Nelson, hit the nail on the head when he said:

> "As far as I know, most organizations are avoiding population issues because they're politically frightened by the charge that comes from some proponents of immigration that if you oppose the immigration policy we have now, you're a racist. There is no way in the world we can forge a sustainable society without stabilizing the population... There's no practical way of stabilizing the population of the U.S. without reducing the immigration

rate. When do we decide we have to do something, or do we wait until things are as bad here as they are in the countries people want to leave?"[xxxix]

Terrorists have an answer to population growth in the U.S.—the mass murder of U.S. citizens. Let's see how our border policies have put out the welcome mat for them...

An Open Invitation to Terrorists

Ninety-three percent of the illegal aliens apprehended at the U.S.—Mexico border are Mexicans, so the U.S. Border Patrol simply divides those they apprehend into two categories — Mexican and "Other than Mexicans," or OTMs. Let's focus on the OTMs for a moment, as this is the population in which we are most likely to find terrorists infiltrating our country.

In 2003, the number of OTMs apprehended was 30,000; in 2004, this number had more than doubled to 76,000, and in 2005, the number had more than doubled again to 155,000.[xl] Remember, these are just the people that are caught, so roughly five times this number have successfully infiltrated our country. Of these, a staggering 20% come from terror-sponsoring countries like Iran, Saudi Arabia, Iraq, Afghanistan, and other Middle Eastern countries.[xli]

If this isn't an argument for controlling our border, I don't know what is. I personally think that if another major terrorist attack kills thousands of U.S. citizens and it is confirmed that the perpetrators crossed the Mexican border into the U.S. to commit their crimes, all of the congressmen who repeatedly voted against border control should be brought up on charges of murder.

So—we're only catching one in five of these potential terrorists crossing into the U.S. over the Mexican border, but at least we are capturing some. If you're like me, you probably picture them sitting in Guantanamo Bay terrorist prisons being "gently" interrogated to find out their plans, right? Well, you'd be dead wrong, I'm afraid. What does the U.S. government actually do with these folks?

When the Border Patrol apprehends Mexican citizens crossing the border, they do not put them in jail. They put them on a bus, drive them back to the border, and turn them loose to try again. That's bad enough. But when it comes to those OTMs, the more likely terrorists, they drive them to an INS processing center in the nearest U.S. city and *turn them loose there.* That's right—they simply release them. Of course, they make them promise to return in a year for a formal hearing. Does anyone out there think the terrorists are likely to return for that hearing? In fact, in a shocking admission, President Bush conceded that only one in five return for the hearing.[xlii] It was a surprise to me that any returned. At any rate, the remaining four are walking around in the U.S., plotting who-knows-what. Well, in some cases we *do* know.

In March of 2005, Lebanon-based Mahmoud Youssef Kourani pled guilty to federal charges stemming from his work in Dearborn, Michigan to raise money for Hezbollah's terrorist activities in Lebanon.[xliii] Kourani bribed a Mexican consular official in Beirut to get him a visa to travel to Mexico (I'll bet that was really hard) to infiltrate via our southern border.

In March 2006, FBI Director Robert Mueller told a House Appropriations sub-committee that the FBI had broken up a Hezbollah smuggling ring in Mexico that was infiltrating Hezbollah operatives into the U.S. across the Mexican border.[xliv]

On an ongoing basis, federal, state and local officials, along with U.S. civilians are finding other evidence of terrorist activities on the border. This evidence includes items such as "discarded beverage boxes with Arabic writing, a jacket with a patch depicting an airliner flying into a tall building followed by the words "Midnight Mission," and an Arabic military patch.[xlv]

There is even evidence of suspected terror training camps operated by the Zetas (former Mexican military special forces who deserted in the mid-1990s) across the river from Brownsville, Texas, where a large number of people are being trained in paramilitary warfare and exotic explosives. Since 9/11, Mexican authorities have reportedly apprehended hundreds of individuals with suspected terrorist ties in the border region.[xlvi]

From my column *Annexing Mexico Revisited,* February, 2006:

> *Going back as far as 2002, news agencies such as the Associated Press, as well as media from the* **New York Times** *to the* **Washington Times** *and* **Town-Hall.com** *have run features citing corruption and collusion on the part of the Mexican police and military, drug cartels, and guess what—now, even our own government.*
>
> *On September 25, 2002, Jerry Seper of the* **Washington Times**

wrote "This isolated area of the U.S.-Mexico border [Sonoyta, Mexico], a 100-mile-wide stretch of wild desert ...has become one of America's newest drug corridors. Mexican drug lords, backed by corrupt Mexican military officers and police officials, will move tons of marijuana, cocaine and heroin this year over rugged desert trails to accomplices in Phoenix and Tucson..."

NewsMax.com, *March 12, 2003; "Mexican Army Invades U.S.," by Phil Brennan: "It's the war nobody wants to talk about: well-armed Mexican soldiers storming across America's southern border, sometimes with guns blazing. 'We are in state of war,' [Edward Nelson, chairman of U.S. Border Control]. 'And we are fighting enemies who have brought the battle to our shores. If ever there was a time for the United States to put troops on the border, it is now.'"*

The New York Times, *July 5, 2005; "Corruption Hampers Mexican Police in Border Drug*

War," by Ginger Thompson: "...this country has been forced to re-examine its police as it struggles against a devastating crime wave that in the last six months has taken more than 600 lives. At least half those killings have happened in the six Mexican states along the border with the United States, where drug traffickers fighting for control of lucrative drug routes empty their automatic weapons on busy streets in the light of day...where powerful cartels took over large parts of the country by corrupting or killing police officers, politicians, journalists and judges."

*And finally, on January 26, 2006, Sarah Carter, a reporter for the **Inland Valley Daily Bulletin** (Ontario, CA), reported in her article (part of an ongoing investigation on border corruption) "Cover-ups of Mexican military border crossings anger agents" that "Some officials suggested Wednesday that the confrontation between Texas law officers earlier this week was with drug smugglers, not Mexican*

*soldiers assisting narcotics traf-
fickers across the Rio Grande.
But a Border Patrol agent who
spoke on condition of anonymity
said continuous cover-ups by
Mexican and U.S. officials have
put many agents and American
lives in danger. 'I think it shows
how desperate the situation has
become. I think it's insulting to
expect Americans to believe what
(Department of Homeland Security Secretary Michael) Chertoff
and the Mexican government are
saying.' "*

The most sobering revelation came on
October 17, 2006, when the House Committee on Homeland Security Subcommit-
tee on Investigations released a lengthy report entitled *A Line in the Sand: Confronting
the Threat at the Southwest Border.* Citing
numerous thoroughly-investigated confron-
tations between Border Patrol agents and
Mexican drug gangs and other criminal elements, two menacing facts surfaced:

1.   Our border Patrol is completely outgunned by the "soldiers" of Mexican drug
cartels operating on the border.
2.   Individuals from terrorist-sponsoring
nations have been freely using this porous

border to infiltrate the United States. A program initiated by Venezuela's proto-human dictator Hugo Chavez that is currently training visitors from terrorist-sponsoring Middle Eastern and Asian nations to speak Spanish and "pose as Latinos" as they entered the U.S., equipped with Venezuelan passports.

Yet, still—anyone—from politician to man-in-the-street—who even *suggests* implementing effective border controls is branded an isolationist bigot by far Left white liberals and naturalized Latino activists. This intimidation, to date, has worked *like a charm.* With all that's at stake, I find this phenomenon disgusting to a degree I cannot describe.

I don't know about you, but the idea of securing our southern border looks more and more attractive to me with each passing day. We'll wrap up this chapter by looking at that border in more detail.

The Border

The U.S. government has responded to public opinion through a cycle of making a show of policing the border. Since the early 1990s, the INS budget has more than tripled, making it the fastest-growing federal agency. In fact, the INS has more personnel authorized to carry a gun than any other federal agency other than the military. Between 1993 and 1999, the number of Border Patrol agents grew from 3,389 to 8,200[xlvii]. In the San Diego sector alone the number of border patrol agents grew from 998 to 2,264. Between this and the Operation Gatekeeper fence in San Diego County you'd think things would be improving.

They're not.

In terms of successful crossings on the first attempt, the rate was 78 percent before January 1995, 87 percent during 1995, and 81 percent in the first half of 1996.[xlviii] Remember, if they don't make it on the first attempt it's nothing more than a minor inconvenience to wait until the following night and try again.

A University of California-San Diego study found that the majority of immigrant-dependent employers in the San Diego had noticed no change in illegal labor availability between before and after Operation Gatekeeper.

What the San Diego fence has done is push the migration paths to the east of the city, where it's more difficult to film the crossings on television. This was a success for the Federal Government, I suppose— but only in the area of public relations.

What about commercial, legal traffic across the border? I'll talk more about this in subsequent chapters, but let me give you an indication of the magnitude of the problem. At the busiest border crossing in the U.S. there are 5,000 trucks entering the United States daily. Border Patrol officials estimate that it would take three men working for five solid hours to thoroughly inspect a single 40-foot cargo container on the back of these trucks. The actual time allocated is 2 minutes.

Our former Secretary of Defense, Casper Weinberger, didn't think the border could be effectively patrolled even with 60,000 full-time troops stationed along its length.[xlix] The border is 2,000 miles long, passing through an area as large as Europe. Much of the border is mountainous, crisscrossed by a maze of mountain ranges. As fast as we build fences they can be torn down, cut through, or tunneled under.

Fortunately, there is an obvious solution. The *southern* border of Mexico is narrow, and Mexico has already done considerable work to fortify this border.

How the United States Became the United States

"Destiny beckons us to hold and civilize Mexico."
Secretary of State James Buchanan, 1846

"Miserable, inefficient Mexico—what has she to do with the great mission of peopling the New World with a noble race? Be it ours to achieve this mission!"

Walt Whitman, 1846

The 2,000 mile long border with Mexico is more than a boundary between two nation states—it is a dividing line between the richest, most powerful nation on earth and (for all practical purposes) a Third World, poverty stricken nation. In fact, it is the only dividing line in the world with this stark contrast. Journalist Robert Kaplan describes the border this way: He recounts traveling between East and west Germany while the Berlin Wall was still up, the Iran-Iraq border with Kurdish rebels, the "Green Line" that separates the antagonistic Greek and Turkish communities on Cyprus, the "Line of Demarcation" between Pakistan and India, and the borders between Damascus, Syria and the demilitarized zone of the Golan Heights. "But never in my life," he says, "have I experienced such a sudden transition as when I crossed from Nogales, Sonora [Mexico] to Nogales, Arizona on November 1st, 1995.[1] We'll revisit the differences between life on one side of the border and life on the other side of the border in the next chapter, but let's look at the border itself a bit more.

The attitude about the border is different from one side of the border to the other. Americans overwhelmingly view the border as a boundary that separates the two countries, and in fact, a significant majority of the population (68 percent) believe so much in that boundary that they agree with the statement "The U.S. should deploy military troops on the border as a temporary measure to help the US Border Patrol curb illegal immigration." In contrast, the same polling agency found that the majority of Mexicans (58 percent) agree with the statement "the territory of the Southwest United States belongs to Mexico." In fact, a popular song in Mexico goes like this (translation by Allan Wall):

*A thousand times they have
shouted at me
'Go home, you don't belong here'
Let me remind the Gringo
That I didn't cross the border, the border crossed me
America was born free—man divided her
They drew the line so we had to jump it
And they call me the invader. . .*

*They purchased from us, without money, the waters of the Río Bravo
They took from us Texas, New Mexico, Arizona, and Colorado
California too and Nevada
Even with Utah it was not enough—they also took Wyoming from us!*

*We are more American than any son of the Anglo-Saxon...
We are more American than every last one of the Gringos.*

45

This issue of changing boundaries certainly bears some analysis. In this chapter we'll look at shifting boundaries of the United States, with a particular emphasis on boundaries with Mexico. We'll look at the evolution of the border with Mexico as a real, versus imaginary, dividing line. We'll also look at changing attitudes toward immigrants throughout the history of the U.S. Finally, we'll look at some relevant history of San Diego and Tijuana as a particular case in point. Let's start with a bit of a history lesson.

We Didn't Start Out with 50 States

> *"The world should be familiarized with the idea of considering our proper domain to be the continent of North America. From the time we became an independent people, it was as much a law of nature that this should become our pretension as that the Mississippi should flow to the sea. Spain had possession of our southern border and Great Britain was upon our north. It is impossible that centuries should elapse without finding their territories annexed to the United States."*

President John Quincy Adams, 1825

Most of us think of the 50 states that make up the United States, and somehow feel like that's what the United States always was. No doubt that our sun-astray educational system has a part in this, but I digress. Sure, most of us recall learning about the 13 colonies, but that doesn't shake our emotional, gut feeling that the current outline of the United States has been, somehow, defined by a higher power. Nothing could be further from the truth. Every bit of the United States was taken from someone else. Now don't get me wrong, I make no apologies for this. We took it because we could, but we successfully kept it because we did more with it than the people we took it from (as we'll discuss further in the next chapter).

For most of our history, there has been an obsession with the physical possession and control of territorial space. Arguments in support of this have ranged from beliefs that "God intended it" (á la Manifest Destiny) to economic motives, as with Charles Conant's argument that imperialism was necessary to absorb the surplice capital in the face of a shortage of profitable investment outlets, or in his words, to relieve the problem of "congested capital."[li]

Our newest two states, Alaska and Hawaii, didn't become states until 1959, within the lifetime of many people reading this book. Alaska was purchased from Russia, and our military was used to help European sugar plantation owners in Hawaii to overthrow the native government[lii]. We tried unsuccessfully to annex Canada in 1812 and the fear of our armies was the primary reason Canada sought, and obtained, independence from Britain (both Canada and Britain judged correctly that we were less likely to make war with an independent Canada). We had better luck to the south.

The first people to "conquer" North America were the Indians, who almost certainly arrived via an ice/land bridge connecting Siberia and Alaska. As far as we know, they were the first humans to set foot on the continent, so in some sense, I guess Russia could claim they were here first and own North America. Certainly, those Siberian descendants have a reasonable claim—that is, if one subscribes to the infantile "whoever got there first should get it back no matter how many eons have passed" dogma.

Unfortunately for them, Europeans arrived and every territorial dispute that of any consequence today involves some European nation claiming (or having once laid claim to) this or that territory. As in nature, the stronger and meaner dog prevails.

Going into 1800, the United States' boundaries were the Mississippi River on the West and the northern border of Florida on the south. France, Spain, Russia, and England had claims to the rest of the continent; indigenous peoples were a nuisance to be controlled or killed.

As Napoleon Bonaparte rose to power, he was able to force Spain to cede "Louisiana" to France in return for lands in Italy. The treaty gave Spain the right of first refusal if France sold the land, but France became concerned about the British taking possession, so in 1803 they sold it to the United States for $15 million without offering Spain the right of refusal. President Thomas Jefferson, God love him, then made the outrageous claim that Louisiana included all lands

49

north of the Rio Grande and east of the Mississippi. In 1808, Napoleon invaded Spain and, in the ensuing confusion, the U.S. invaded western Florida. Spain was a bit slow to relinquish Florida to us, so in 1818 we invaded eastern Florida as well to force their hand. In 1819, Spain came to the bargaining table, as it were, and agreed to give us all of Florida along with what is now Washington, Oregon, and Idaho in exchange for a cash payment (which was never made) and our recognition of a southern boundary that gave Spain what is now Texas, Arizona, Utah, Nevada, California, and half of Colorado.

"Manifest Destiny" was the policy that held to the idea that the United States had a mission to expand, spreading its form of democracy and freedom. Its advocates believed that the United States' occupancy of the entire North American continent was essentially its "destiny".

Many in the United States were therefore unhappy with the 1819 treaty, believing that it superseded Manifest Destiny. In 1823 Mexico gained independence from Spain, although the dominant class throughout Mexico remained Spanish citizens (just as the dominant class in the United States was British). At this time, President James Monroe declared that the Americas (North and South) were off limits

to European interven-
tion, a policy known as
the Monroe Doctrine.

During the early
1800s, there was a ma-
jor problem with illegal
aliens crossing the U.S.-
Mexico boundary. The
illegal aliens retained
their own language and
customs and refused to
assimilate. Eventually
they had enough critical mass to enable
them to declare a new, independent homeland. In this case, the border crossers were
American citizens who were crossing into
Mexico and the new homeland was the Republic of Texas. Between 1836 and 1845,
Texas existed in this independent status,
until President John Tyler annexed Texas
into the United States in 1845, thus infuri-
ating Mexico. At this time, the southern
border of Texas was the
Nueces River, but the
U.S. maintained that
the boundary was 150
miles to the south at the
Rio Grande.

The next U.S. presi-
dent, James Polk, saw
an opportunity to se-
cure additional territory

(especially, Arizona, Utah, Nevada, and California). He sent US troops down to the Rio Grande, which Mexico saw as a U.S. invasion. A full scale war ensued. Two years later, 6,000 U.S. soldiers had taken over Mexico City. At this point Polk could have taken all of Mexico and been done with it, but much like George H.W. Bush in Iraq, he got cold feet. Instead, the Treaty of Guadalupe-Hidalgo was negotiated in which Mexico ceded one million square miles of land, an area equivalent in size to Western Europe and equal to one-half of its territory, to the United States. All or part of Texas, Arizona, New Mexico, Oklahoma, Wyoming, Colorado, Kansas, Utah, Nevada, and California thus became part of the United States. In 1853, the Gadsden Purchase was negotiated giving the U.S. an area the size of Connecticut, Massachusetts, and Rhode Island combined for $10 million. The United States' primarily concern at the time was building a transcontinental railroad, and the acquisition of this real estate facilitated this objective nicely. Apparently, Mexico had no stomach for playing hardball at this juncture, as they offered to throw in Baja California for an additional $10 million. The shortsighted Congress turned the offer down.

The Border as a Boundary

"Generally speaking, every human-made boundary on the earth's surface—garden hedge, city wall, or radar "fence"—is an attempt to keep inimical forces at bay. Boundaries are everywhere because threats are ubiquitous: the neighbor's dog, children with muddy shoes, strangers, the insane, alien armies, disease, wolves, wind and rain."

Yi-Fu Tuan
Landscapes of Fear

It is time to face the facts: Anglos won't go back to Europe, and Mexicans and Latinos (legal or illegal) won't  *go back to Latin America. We are all here to stay. For better or for worse, our destinies and aspirations are in one another's hands. For me, the only solution lies in a paradigm shift: the recognition*

53

that we are all protagonists in the creation of a new cultural topography and a new social order, one in which we all are 'others,' and we need the 'others' to exist. Hybridity is no longer up for discussion. It is a demographic, racial, social, and cultural fact."

Guillermo Gómez-Peña,
The New World Border

The idea of controlled borders between nations is a relatively new phenomenon in history. Political entities traditionally envisioned their sovereignty as being over subjects rather than over specific geographic territory. In the sixteenth century, the concept of territorial sovereignty and nation began to emerge, but even as late as the end of the nineteenth century border controls and passports were largely unknown in Europe.

Until World War I, the only issue regarding people crossing the U.S.-Mexico border was Mexico's repeated requests that we control the border to prevent raids by "filibusters" from Texas and California into Mexico, hoping to "liberate" northern Mexico. The outbreak of World War I led the U.S. to implement travel restrictions and to deploy troops along the border. It was during this time that discussions began about forming a permanent Border Patrol, and in fact, the Immigration Act of 1924 created the U.S. border Patrol with an initial budget of $1 million.

The unauthorized entry of Mexicans into the U.S. was a non-issue for U.S. authorities, however. According to people who lived in the border region at the time, people could cross from Tijuana into San Diego "as if a border did not exist" as late as 1930. Most of the border with Mexico was nothing more than an occasional stone pillar here and there. Unauthorized immigration was of such little concern that the only reason San Diego congressman James Utt gave for building a ten mile border fence was to prevent diseased Mexican cattle from crossing the border and infecting the U.S. dairy herds.

Even with the passage of the Immigration Act of 1917, Mexicans were exempted. By about the time of World War II, attitudes had changed and the *Bracero* program was created, admitting but controlling Mexican guest workers. When an illegal immigrant was found working in the U.S., the Border Patrol would take them to a processing station and fill out the paperwork to make them legal under this program, a process known as "drying out the wetback." For those who say that it would be impossible to deport all of the illegal aliens currently in the U.S., you don't need to go back any further than 1953-1955 when the nation responded to an agricultural slowdown by deporting over 2 million of these Bracero program guest workers. Ironically, ten years later, it was Mexico that restricted travel by United States citizens, prohibiting "hippies" and men with long hair from entering Tijuana for fear that they were influencing Mexican citizens with their anti-work attitudes and sloppy dress.

Spanish missionaries established their first mission in California in San Diego in 1769, and San Diego had remained a small mission town. At the time, the Treaty of Guadalupe Hidalgo was signed in 1848, putting San Diego in the U.S. and Tijuana in Mexico, the total population of San Diego was 350, and Tijuana was even smaller.

Both cities have grown rapidly over the past 150 years, but while San Diego is now one of the most beautiful cities in the world, Tijuana remains a third-world border region with inadequate roads, sewer, water, education, vaccinations, etc. Generally speaking, the resources are the same, the people are the same, yet few would deny that all else being equal, someone born in San Diego starts life off much better than someone born in Tijuana.

What's different? The government of the United States versus the government of Mexico, of course. We'll explore this further in the next chapter.

The Rights of Man

We hold these Truths to be self-evident, that all Men are created equal, that they are endowed, by their Creator, with certain unalienable Rights, that among these are Life, Liberty, and the Pursuit of Happiness.

That to secure these Rights, Governments are instituted among Men, deriving their just Powers from the Consent of the Governed, that whenever any Form of Government becomes destructive of these Ends, it is the Right of the People to alter or abolish it, and to institute new Government, laying its Foundation on such Principles, and organizing its Powers in such Form, as to them shall seem most likely to effect their Safety and Happiness.

> *...when a long Train of Abuses and Usurpations, pursuing invariably the same Object, evinces a Design to reduce them under absolute Despotism, it is their Right, it is their Duty, to throw off such Government, and to provide new Guards for their future Security.*
>
> —Preamble to the
> Declaration of Independence

The Preamble is almost identical to *The Declaration of the Rights of Man* by Thomas Paine (1789). Fundamentally, the core philosophy of both is that the government exists to serve the people, not the other way around. When a government has proven that it does not serve the people, but is in fact harmful to the people, then it is the right *and duty* of those people to replace the government. In this chapter, we'll look at the following fundamental question, "Would the people of Mexico be better off remaining citizens of an independent Mexico, or would they be better off as citizens of a United States which stretched from the Canadian border to Central America? Fret not; in later chapters we'll be looking at the related question: "Would the people of the United States be better off with Mexico as part of the United States, or as an independent country?"

Mexico is a nation rich in natural resources; were in not for this, the nation would more resemble Cuba or Haiti. That the oppressed *mestizo* and *indio* population have the option of a relatively "convenient" way out is for them, in a practical sense, a profound blessing.

Mexicans are generally also a hard-working, family-oriented population. There is nothing fundamentally different about San Diego versus Tijuana, so why are the people on one side of the border so much better off than the people on the other side of the border?

Jim Crow in Mexico?
Say it ain't so!

> *"Mexican migrants do jobs that not even blacks want to do."*
> - Former Mexican President
> Vicente Fox

I contend that the fault of class disparity falls 100% on the side of the Mexican government. Further, due to the ingrained governmental corruption, the problems are not ones that can be fixed by electing new leaders. They are endemic to their government at all levels (the federal, state, and city) and to their legal system. The problem started with the formation of Mexico, which was based on a class hierarchy with Spaniards at the top, followed by individuals descended from Spanish parents but born in Mexico (*criollos*), then those of mixed Indian and Spanish blood (*mestizos*), with native Indians (*indios*) and Africans at the bottom. The only protection offered to the underprivileged was what was granted by the powerful—there was no judicial system. This class hierarchy is still found in Mexico, where the poorest of the poor are the native Indians and the richest are the *criollos.* In terms of cultural development and concepts of human rights, it is clear that Mexico is somewhere between 50 and 150 years behind the United States. You won't see any *mestizos* or *indios* holding high public office—or any *criollos* wading across the Rio Grande.

If anyone wants proof that the whole system doesn't work, just take a drive through the country. Open ditch sewers still dominate the rural areas, dogs run loose in dirt streets, bandits rob tourists and businessmen alike, tourists are kidnapped, and sewage flows untreated into streams. In a report prepared in the mid-1980s it was estimated that forty-four tons of hazardous *maquilador* waste per day went unaccounted for. There is a five-year difference in average life expectancy between someone living on the U.S. side of the border and someone living on the Mexican side of the border.[liii]

Listen to how journalist Robert Kaplan contrasts a U.S. border city with the Mexican border city a few hundred yards away:

> *The billboards, sidewalks, traffic markers, telephone and electric cable, and so on appeared straight, and all their curves and angles uniform... The store logos were made of expensive polymers rather than cheap plastic. I heard no metal rattling in the wind. The cars were the same makes I had seen in Mexico, but oh how different: no more chewed-up, rusted bodies; no more cracked windshields held together by black tape; no more crosses and other good-luck charms hanging inside the windshields; no more noise from broken mufflers. The taxi I entered on the U.S. side had shock absorbers. The neutral gray upholstery was not shredded. The meter printed out receipts.*[liv]

The hotel he patronized in the U.S. charged the same rate as the hotel in Mexico, which was only two years old. But the hotel in Mexico was already falling apart: "The doors didn't close properly, the paint was cracking, the walls were beginning to stain" while the hotel on the American side was 25 years old but in "excellent condition."

Perhaps the most disturbing problem of all is the rampant corruption through all aspects of society in Mexico. A saying in Mexico goes, "If you get mugged don't yell, you may attract the police." People are stopped on trumped up charges and held until a "ransom" is paid by relatives, if they're released at all. Ask anyone living in San Diego who travels to Mexico regularly and they will either have a personal experience with corruption in Mexico, or they will personally know someone who has had such an experience. An entire battalion of the Mexican army had to be disbanded when more than six hundred members of the battalion were found protecting poppy and marijuana crops.[lv] Levels of violence and police corruption in Nuevo Laredo, across the border from Laredo, Texas, reached the point in 2005 where the Mexican government was forced to suspend the entire Nuevo Laredo police force. After the new police chief was assassinated only hours after his appointment, 305 of the town's 765 police were dismissed and 41 were arrested for attacking the federal law enforcement officials. Also in 2005, prosecutors charged 27 states, federal and local police in Cancun with running a drug ring and/or aiding in the murder of fellow police officers.[lvi]

One example of the problem is the use of *Madrinas.* Officially recognized Mexican government employees are known as *funcionarios.* These funcionarios then appoint others to act on their behalf. These appointees are the Madrinas. Thus, they have the power of the funcionarios but not the accountability. They draw no salary, but live from the *mordida,* or bribes that they collect and share with their funcionarios. There are many advantages to employing Madrinas, including:

• There is no payroll.

• There are no records. Officially, Madrinas don't exist.

• If there are complications of any sort, Madrinas are expendable.

• In serious cases of corruption or malfeasance, when someone must be identified and punished, Madrinas can be scapegoats. They can be murdered, and an official can be portrayed as the hero for ending the problem.

• If Madrinas are apprehended in the possession of government equipment (military vehicles, weapons, supplies, clothing, documents), they can be labeled as thieves and counterfeiters.

• Madrinas do the dirty work so the authorities can remain above reproach.

• Madrinas are usually chosen from the most brutal, morally depraved, meanest individuals in the community. Many have criminal records and have been imprisoned in the United States, Mexico, or both.[lvii]

Mexico is one of the poorest countries in the world, but the rich in Mexico are *very* rich. Mexico is ranked fourth worldwide in the number of billionaires, right behind the U.S., Japan and Germany. Meanwhile, nearly half the population lives in poverty and twenty-five percent of the population lives in abject poverty.[lviii] Mexico has a population of 105 million with a per capita gross domestic product (GDP) of only $5,877. In comparison, the per capita GDP of the United States is $36,067.[lix] The

THE RIGHTS OF MAN

U.S. GDP per person is six times greater than that in the Mexico.

One big reason for the discrepancy is investments. Economists use the ratio of investments to GDP measure the extent to which a country is reinvesting in its development. Investments are defined as expenditures on relatively long lasting goods and services that increase the ability of the economy to produce more goods and services. Most countries vary between 20 and 40 percent, with fully developed countries at the low end of this range and newly industrializing economies at the high end of this range. For example, as a fully industrialized country this number for the US is 21 percent. Canada is working (successfully) to narrow the income gap with the US with a score of 26. Throughout the period of 1979–1991 China remained in the range of 36 to 38, and they are currently a staggering 45, which also explains why they are the fastest growing economy in the world. Throughout the past 25 years, Mexico has hovered in the 16 percent range.

If you want a more specific example of shortsighted thinking having negative financial consequences, you need look no further than Pemex. Mexico has huge oil reserves. Mexico nationalized their oil industry in 1938 and created the resultant government monopoly Pemex. Today, in spite of record oil prices Pemex continues to operate at a loss.

The problems in Mexico are so severe that the best option appears to be for them to start over—with our help.

The people of Mexico obviously agree. In a survey, 70 percent of Mexicans said that they would "vote with their feet" and immigrate to the United States if they were permitted and thought they would benefit economically.[lx] Given that ten to twenty percent of the population of Mexico is already living in the United States illegally I think that the mandate is pretty clear. Ninety-four percent of Americans believe that "our society should do what is necessary to make sure that everyone has an equal opportunity to succeed."[lxi] There are 100 million people south of our border that do not have anything like an equal opportunity to succeed in life. If we just opened our borders, Mexico would be left with the ten percent of the population who are in that rarified upper strata and everyone else would be over here.

I have a better idea. Instead of leaving Mexico desolate and abandoned, let's bring the United States to them!

We All Win

"One of the strengths of this country has been our diversity. One of the strengths of this country has been the fact that we are a nation of immigrants."
—Christine Whitman
Former Governor, New Jersey

"There is no room in this country for hyphenated Americanism. When I refer to hyphenated Americans, I do not refer to naturalized Americans. Some of the very best Americans I

*have ever known were natural-
ized Americans, Americans born
abroad. But a hyphenated
American is not an American at
all. This is just as true of the
man who puts "native" before
the hyphen as of the man who
puts German or Irish or English
or French before the hyphen.
Americanism is a matter of the
spirit and of the soul. Our allegiance must be purely to the
United States. We must unspar-
ingly condemn any man who
holds any other allegiance."*
—President Theodore Roosevelt

The views of President Roosevelt and Governor Whitman are not mutually exclusive.
They are not even at odds with each other.
The United States has a significant capacity to absorb and assimilate immigrants to
the benefit of both. But assimilation is the
key. The reason each of the territorial ex-
pansions of the U.S. was ultimately successful is that in each case the people living in that area where assimilated. They
became Americans, not hyphenated Americans. I believe that the only feasible way to
solve the immigration issues in this country is to assimilate Mexico into the United
States so completely that we no longer

have Mexican-Americans, legal or otherwise—we just have Americans.

Fortunately, Mexico has a wealth of resources to bring to the table. Let's start by looking at oil.

The second largest oil-producing complex in the world is Mexico's Cantarell oil field in the gulf of Mexico. Scientists believe that this field was created 65 million years ago when the Chicxulub meteor impacted the Earth. As is too often the case, future industrial progress came at the expense of massive extinctions—of dinosaurs in this case. In 2006, Mexico announced the discovery of a second huge oil field, the Noxal field off the coast of Veracruz. This new field could well be larger than Cantarell. Mexico is already one of the world's largest producers of oil, and this new find could double that production. Mexico is already the second most important source of US oil, behind only Canada, and there is no reason they couldn't be a significant part of a strategy of North American energy independence.

That's right. It's not that far-fetched to see North America as oil-independent after all. Now let's look at petroleum reserves for the top oil-producing countries.

Mexico is blessed with a wide variety of other resources, but perhaps her next greatest asset after oil is her hard working people. Border factories, called *Maquiladoras*, rank with oil among the top producers of revenue for Mexico.

Mexico is already the top destination for U.S. tourists with 20 million visitors (Canada was second with 13 million, and the United Kingdom was a distant third with 2.3 million). If problems with crime and corruption were solved the tourist industry would offer unlimited potential to tourists from around the world.

The business world has largely treated North America as a single entity for many years now. North America is considered to be largest of the three major trading areas within the world, with the other two being the European Union (EU) and the Asia-Pacific (ACPAC) trading region. By way of comparison, in 1999 the North American Gross Domestic Product (GDP) was $10 trillion, versus $8.3 trillion for the European Union.

Surprisingly, the degree to which the three countries of North America are already integrated is quite high. Canada and Mexico are the number one and two trading partners of the United States. Trade between the United States and Mexico exceeds $250 billion per year. Mexico ships 90 percent of its exports to the United States and obtains 70 percent of its imports from the United States.[lxii] More than

85 percent of Mexico's exports to the U.S. are manufactured goods. Each year more than 300 million people, 90 million cars, and 4.3 million trucks legally cross the border between the United States and Mexico.[lxiii]

Another way of looking at this is that less than 1 percent of all people crossing the border are doing so illegally. An estimated 50,000 Tijuana, Mexico residents legally work at jobs in San Diego, commuting back and forth across the border each day.[lxiv] NAFTA has been largely responsible for the huge growth in trade between the three North American countries. Since the onset of NAFTA trade between all combinations of countries within NAFTA has shot up, along with foreign direct investment (FDI) between the countries.[lxv] NAFTA may be credited with the creation of more than twenty million net jobs (jobs gained minus jobs lost) in the three countries. Unfortunately, the governments shortchanged the people of North America by limiting NAFTA to issues of commerce.

If the three countries of North America were roughly equivalent with each other, then the most logical course of action would be a European Union style arrangement. Each of the three countries would maintain autonomy over internal matters but there would be external cooperation on regional issues such as security, commerce, currency, free movement of labor, and so on. In fact, this type of arrangement might be just the ticket between the United States and Canada.

Unfortunately, Mexico is simply too far behind the power curve for this to work. Their infrastructure is practically non-existent. The education system is largely non-existent in rural areas and of extremely poor quality in most places. Third world diseases abound. The legal system is incompatible. Corruption abounds. As much as many internationalists and Latino activists would like to, we can't just open our borders with conditions being the way they are now. We need to bring Mexico up to something approximating the level of the United States and Canada, and the only effective way to do that is by using a plan more similar to the reunification of East and West Germany than an EU-type model.

Yes—I know this all sounds monumentally condescending and politically incorrect—but the facts speak for themselves. Were this not true, Mexicans wouldn't go through so much trouble to come here in the first place.

There are many benefits to both the U.S. and Mexico of making Mexico part of the United States and gradually bringing

Mexico up to the standards of other developed Western nations. Let's examine some of the more obvious advantages.

It will be much easier to control our southern border when the greatest source of illegal immigration, Mexico, is no longer a factor. Perhaps most significant, we can finally get tough on illegal immigration, and radically slow down legal immigration as well, without offending a significant percentage of our voting population. In fact, I would recommend a heavily fortified and patrolled border at the south of Mexico, temporary reduction in legal immigration, strong enforcement efforts to deport any illegal, non-Mexican immigrants living in the country, and clarification that children born in the U.S. to non-U.S. citizens will no longer be eligible for automatic U.S. citizenship.

None of this is feasible, however, as long as Mexico is so integrated into our country, but all of this becomes feasible once Mexico is part of our country. This would significantly improve the security of both countries and make it more difficult for terrorists to use this as an entry vehicle.

The government could then implement U.S. sanitation standards and health policies, vaccinating our newest citizens and slowly eliminating the third world diseases that threaten Mexico (and us) today.

We could upgrade the school system in Mexico, especially in rural areas, educating the work force and instilling American values. It burns me up to pay for schooling the children of another country, but I'd be the first in line to pay for the schooling of the new citizens of the U.S. southern territories. The EU faced a similar problem with schooling, especially in rural areas within Spain and Portugal. With EU help Spain and Portugal established small colleges in rural provinces. These colleges attracted professionals and served as an influence on education at all levels. As a result, the proportion of students in higher education in Spain increased from 29 to 48 percent; and in Portugal, from 12 to 39 percent and over the same period of time *all* high school-age students in Portugal and Spain were in school. Mexico is currently about where Portugal was at the start of this process, with 15 percent of its students in higher education and 61 percent of high school age students actually in high school.

Of course, barriers to investment, travel, and so on would disappear. Over time the minimum wage in Mexico would rise to match the minimum wage in the

U.S. and working conditions would improve to meet OSHA standards.

Removing corruption from the government, police, and so on would take time and involve education and changing the climate of corruption. This might be the greatest challenge, but I'm sure that it is possible. In a culture in which bribery and graft were acceptable, it's hard to justify punishing someone now for taking a bribe last year. But there must be a dividing line going forward, and taking bribes or other illegal activities past that point must be punished.

Drugs are a big part of the problem, leading to much of the most violent criminal activity. Having Mexico subject to U.S. law and internal law enforcement efforts would help somewhat, but a heavy hand would have to be wielded against the well-established renegade police and military who enforce for many drug gangs, and the drug gangs themselves.

With improved standards of living and education combined with reduced immigration from outside of North America, it should be possible to achieve zero net population growth throughout the United States, something that is still an important goal for ecological reasons. In fact, resuming external immigration should be tied to achieving this goal, and the number of immigrants allowed should be restricted to ensure no net population growth. Of course, our environmental concerns and programs would be initiated throughout Mexico to help ensure accountability for hazardous waste, air pollution standards, and so on.

Through a combination of efficient use of North American oil resources and energy conservation efforts it should be possible for North America to become energy independent during this same period of time, with the added benefit of a corresponding reduction in greenhouse gases. In fact, simply moving from low mileage vehicles to high mileage hybrid vehicles that have the added capability of plugging into the electrical grid overnight and driving on electric power alone for the first 50 to 100 miles (pluggable hybrid electric vehicles, or PHEVs) would more-or-less achieve this goal today.

So, if both the people of Mexico and the people of the United States would benefit from the annexation of Mexico, is it time to send in the Marines to finish what we started in 1848? We'll look at this question in the next chapter.

Send in the Marines

I don't think there is any doubt that our military could conquer Mexico in a matter of weeks, if not days. But we don't need to look any further than the example of Iraq to recognize that winning the initial military battle doesn't necessarily mean that the "war" is won.

Fortunately, military force is neither necessary nor desired to accomplish our mutual objectives here. In fact, Mexico's former President Fox called on the U.S. to consider working toward a goal of open borders and mutual security. In fact, 56.2 percent of Mexicans are already in favor of joining the United States in a new amalgamated nation if that would improve their quality of life (versus 31.5 percent opposed), and 30 percent are in favor of being directly annexed into the United States. Support for a single North American country is also high among the U.S. public.[lxvi] It's little wonder: the Mexican census found that with 10% of the population of Mexico living in the U.S., residents from more than 96 percent of all Mexican municipalities have contact with relatives in the United States. In spite of the recent "immigration wars," on the whole the attitudes of Mexicans toward the U.S., and Americans toward the Mexicans are extremely positive. The Chicago Council on Foreign Relations has been studying public perceptions of different countries every four years since 1974. During the past 25 years, Americans have consistently given Canada, the United Kingdom, and Mexico the highest rating of all countries and Mexicans have an equally high opinion of the United States. In fact, approximately 75% of Mexicans have a favorable opinion of the United States and approximately 75% of Americans have a favorable opinion of Mexico. More than 80 percent of Mexicans believe that the United States exercises the most influence on their country, and 67 percent of Mexicans view the U.S. influence as positive[lxvii]—it's only the Latino activists with ties to Marxist U.S.-based groups we see protesting (in the U.S.) and bellowing about U.S. oppression, injustice, racism and other such twaddle.

Mexican national pride

No such animal. The only people you're going to hear bleat about Mexican national pride are:

1. American liberals

2 U.S.-born Latino activists indoctrinated by the above

3. Wealthy Mexican *criollos* (individuals descended from Spaniards)

If in doubt, I'll once again cite the poll released on August 16, 2005 by the Pew Hispanic Center, which indicated that more than 40 percent of Mexican adults would move to the U.S. if they could.

One might argue that black slaves fought on the side of the Confederacy and that blacks fought courageously during World War II and the Korean War despite Jim Crow laws still being in place. One might maintain that they had a sense of national pride, and they might be right.

I would point out two facts concerning that argument:

1. When you've been indoctrinated into a culture for generations, you go with what you know. To the oppressed blacks, it was

81

still their country, however politically and socially inequitable.

2. The oppressed blacks concerned *didn't have a way out similar to that which Mexican immigrants enjoy.*

My point is that these *(mestizos* and *indios)* are an oppressed underclass (sort of like black people used to be), and that is why the majority head north and a near majority would stay here if they could.

Finally, I see nothing wrong with an ethnic group celebrating their *heritage*— but for Mexican émigrés and naturalized Mexicans *(chicanos)* to defend the Mexican government over the American government is akin to native Cubans defending Castro.

I don't think it would take that much effort for the majority of Mexicans to embrace the concept of annexation. Before we examine this in more depth however, let's briefly look at alternatives to annexation.

Areas of Integration

There are five main areas wherein two countries can choose to integrate with each other:

1.   Commerce and Trade;

2.   Security cooperation;

3.   Economic integration;

4.   Legal integration;

5.   Political association.

NAFTA involves integration of commerce and trade. The jury is still out on its long-term effects; some maintain that this integration has been a resounding success for all concerned; others contend that it has adversely affected American farmers, the U.S. job market, trade unions and brought about unintended consequences such as the abuse of women in south-of-the-border sweatshops. There is no doubt that NAFTA has created jobs and offered economic advantages for all three countries. The lingering unanswered question is the cost/benefit ratio.

Security cooperation involves both military cooperation (which is not so much of an issue within North America) and coordinated control of information and people within the countries to prevent terrorist activities. The concept involves control and management of people coming into cooperating national entities, thereby avoiding the need to control the movement of people therein.

Needless to say, we do *not* have effective security cooperation with Mexico.

Economic integration involves combining currencies, combining or coordinating fiscal policies, and so on. Taxation might be implemented to provide funds for projects that would benefit multiple countries, for example.

Legal integration involves establishing compatible and coordinated laws and courts. Legal integration is particularly necessary for full commercial integration.

Political integration involves common or coordinated legal systems, government operations, and foreign policy.

The European Union is an example of the first three, with some limited integration in the last two areas. The United States itself is an example of full integration across all five areas. Let's look at that briefly:

Federal law prohibits most restrictions by states on interstate trade. There are no protective tariffs charged by one state on the goods sold by another state. Basically, people in the U.S. can buy or sell things anywhere within the U.S. that they like. However, individual states are able to have local regulations over things like the amount of sales tax charged (if any).

Individual states have responsibility for maintaining order within their borders, but when they cannot or will not do so, the Federal government has the legal option of intervening. The Federal government has full responsibility for maintaining security of the states against foreign forces. In addition, the Federal government has its own law enforcement agencies that are responsible for enforcing federal laws across state boundaries.

All states use a common currency, and things like exchange rate and federal reserve lending rates are consolidated. However, states are responsible for balancing their own budgets.

There are dual legal systems, state and federal. The state legal systems enforce state laws while the federal legal systems enforce federal laws. However, all use a compatible approach to the law based on a combination of legislation and case law.

Again, there are dual systems when it comes to political models, with each state having its own constitution, political agencies, legislative bodies and so on.

The system is quite flexible and offers a lot of autonomy to the individual states. This form of government is called a Republic. It's exactly this flexibility that makes the integration of Mexico with the U.S. feasible. *Individual states within Mexico would be able to retain a significant amount of autonomy as part of the United States.*

I readily concede that the U.S. Government is not perfect. For example, there are something like 67 different highway transportation standards, many incompatible with each other, for trucks. It would be nice to fix this mess. It's tough to defend the U.S. tax code, something so complicated that even its authors can't understand it. In fact, it is estimated that it costs taxpayers $225 billion for tax filing, tax record keeping, and tax reduction advice alone (that's *before* actual payment of taxes, folks). This might be the perfect time to replace the current income tax mess with a simplified flat tax or consumption based national sales tax. I'm sure there are other abysmal aspects of our governmental bureaucracy that could be revamped as we began to officially assimilate our friends down south.

The integration of Mexico into the United States is not something that could happen overnight. It would be a slow process, possibly taking ten years or longer. One issue that's likely to come up is language.

This is a hot button with many people. People are concerned that the U.S. will transition from an English-only country to one where Spanish is the preeminent language in portions of the country. After annexation, we would certainly have a significant number of people and land where Spanish is the primary or the only language. There are, in fact, still many ethnic neighborhoods in America (several in New York spring to mind) where one is hard-pressed to find people who speak English.

Myth: Mexicans are currently coming to the U.S. and, unlike previous immigrants, refusing to learn English. It simply isn't happening. For first generation Hispanics born in California, 90 percent have native fluency in English and by the second generation only 50 percent speak Spanish at all.[lxviii] In fact, English has become so important in Mexico that the Mexican government established a "National Commission of the Defense of the Spanish Language" to protect Spanish from the encroachment of English in three "disaster" zones:

1.   Mexico City, Guadalajara, and Monterrey;

2.   Centers of tourism, and

3.   Northern border cities.

I believe that (propaganda notwithstanding) a majority of the population in the United States agree that English is the most important language for success worldwide.

Nearly all of Europe (save France), Scandinavia, and even many African nations do.

On the other hand, in today's global economy, the fact that most Americans speak *only* English is pretty ridiculous. There's a joke that made the rounds in Europe a while back that went like this:

What do you call someone who speaks two languages?
Answer: Bi-lingual

What do you call someone who speaks three languages?
Answer: Tri-lingual

What do you call someone who speaks only one language?
Answer: American

Ouch. I'd suggest that we deal with the language issue as follows:

1. English would be the official language of the United States, used for all official functions including education.

2. All children would be taught Spanish as a second language in grade school.

3. To receive a four-year degree from a University, students must either learn or

demonstrate proficiency in a third language of their choice.

With this approach we would retain the world standard language of business, English, as our national language. We would enjoy the cultural diversity of conversational ability in Spanish. And for our University graduates we would enhance our global competitiveness with knowledge of a wide range of other languages.

So how would this annexation be accomplished? I suggest that one of the first steps would be a national vote of the citizens of Mexico, including both those living in the United States and those living in Mexico. It should be clear that non-U.S. citizens will be expelled from the U.S., will not receive economic benefits in this country, and will not be birthing "shake 'n take", instant U.S. citizen children here. It should also be clear that immigration policies going forward will be very restrictive.

The question is, are the people of Mexico willing to be U.S. citizens or not? I do not think it would be difficult to demonstrate the advantage of unification to the majority of Mexican people. I would suggest independently monitored voting on the issue.

Would the U.S. military come into play? Hopefully, they wouldn't. But if the Mexican government refused to go along with the will of the people, I wouldn't hesitate to back the people of Mexico in their rightful overthrow of a corrupt government.

It is clear that the entire idea won't work unless Mexico makes rapid progress from a third-world country to an economic equal with the United States and Canada. The best hope, however, for Mexico to accomplish this is indeed to opt *for* annexation.

The two most formidable challenges will be the reformation of Mexico's education and infrastructure. I've already discussed an approach to improving the education of the Mexican population modeled on that followed in Spain and Portugal by the EU. There would also need to be massive improvements in the Mexican infrastructure. The roads, rail, ports, and telecommunications all need massive development. We would need to be willing to make these investments in the short-term in order to reap the long-term benefits. In the next chapter, I'll attempt to quantify the magnitude of the investment that would be required to make this work—and the long-term economic benefits for both sides.

Who Pays the Bill?

Let's start by recognizing that *we're already paying the bill*. As discussed in the first chapter of this book, we're already paying huge bills for education, medical treatment, incarceration, and other public services for immigrants, legal and otherwise. If Mexico remains the inefficient, ineffective and corrupt nation it currently is, we will continue to receive the overflow and pay the bill, with no return on that investment. By "we", I am of course excluding the shortsighted business interests that benefit in the short term via employing illegal immigrants.

Instead, we can make the investment needed to develop Mexico into an integral part of the United States, then reap the benefit of a vastly expanded economy of producers and consumers, all with a vested interest in the success of the effort. Let's start by looking at some of the more significant costs that we can anticipate.

In the last chapter I mentioned that one of the most significant investment areas that would have to be addressed in order to increase Mexico's pace of development and to facilitate the integration of the two countries was infrastructure development. The World Bank estimates that Mexico will need $20 billion in financing for infrastructure development during the coming decade, or $2 billion per year.[lxix] I speculate that effectively accomplishing our mission of effective assimilation will require double this number, or $4 billion per year for the next 10 years. Total cost, $40 billion in public expenditures (not that much when one considers the daily expense of the Iraq campaign or the current public tab for illegals). I would anticipate that contracts could easily be put in place to support private infrastructure development in areas such as telecommunications and public transportation to support this developing market, and I have not included these private investments in above total figure, although I would expect the private investments to at least match the public investments. I believe that the easing of bureaucratic restrictions and corruption that currently exists in Mexico would lead to a veritable entrepreneurial bonanza for those on both sides of the border.

Enhanced education opportunities will likely prove to be the single largest expense we can anticipate. A commitment to educating the populace requires investment over many years before the students enter the workforce. We should be able to establish an educational system in Mexico that operates similarly to that which existed in the U.S. during the 1950s.

Now, I realize this raises the issue of the relatively abysmal turn the education of students in America has taken over the last 40 years. For the purposes of this book, of course, this is an outside issue, but one that I believe capable and practical minds will one day be able to solve, provided they can get around our increasingly socialist Congress.

Specifically, we can ensure that the majority of funds go to the classroom rather than having the vast majority of the money siphoned off by various layers of bureaucracy and administration. Focusing on private investment would facilitate this nicely, since such enterprises are market-driven (It might even provide useful precedents that could be adapted for U.S. schools).

In today's dollars, the spending per student per year during the 1950s was about $1,700.[lxx] In Mexico, roughly one-quarter of the population is school age, resulting in a school enrollment of 26.6 million.[lxxi] This gives us a total educational requirement of approximately $45 billion dollars per year. In fact, the current Mexican education budget is $45 billion U.S. dollars per year, and their literacy rates are actually higher than the literacy rates of students in US schools. So where's the problem? The Mexican enrollment in secondary schools is 5.8 million but roughly 40% of their population does not finish secondary school. Their enrollment in post-secondary schools is a scant 2.3 million. This is where the majority of investment is required. Let's assume an additional 10% of total education budget, or $4.5 billion dollars per year over ten years, so $45 billion total over ten years to reinforce incentives in this area.

For medical expenditures, let's focus on preventive medicine designed to eradicate third world diseases within Mexico within a generation. This basically involves improved sanitation and vaccinations. Suppose we budget $10 per person as a one-time expense to vaccinate everyone in Mexico. That's $1 billion. Let's add another $2 billion per year over ten years to bring the sewer and water systems up to modern standards. We're now at $3 billion in the first year and $2 billion for the next nine years, or $21 billion total over ten years.

One of the causes of corruption in Mexico is that the public officials are not paid enough to live on, with the implied expectation that they will make up the difference with bribes. Well, these folks must be paid a decent wage if we're going to expect them to stop taking bribes. Law enforcement costs to prosecute those who remain corrupt will be incurred. This is a difficult figure to quantify, but let's assume we needed to budget $4 billion per year for this over the next 10 years, or $40 billion total.

The cost side of the equation now looks something like this:

	1st Year	Years 1-9	Total (10 Yr)
Infrastructure Development	4.0	4.0	40.0
Educational Development	4.5	4.5	45.0
Medical	3.0	2.0	21.0
Remove corruption	4.0	4.0	40.0
	$ 15.50	$ 14.50	$ 146.00

($ in billions)

So we're looking at a ten-year cost of $146 billion dollars, or roughly $15 billion dollars per year. Even if we doubled the figures to $30 billion dollars per year for ten years (or $300 billion dollars total) to annex Mexico and bring it up to something approaching the standards of other developed Western nations over a ten year period, this investment is on a par with what the EU found was required to bring Ireland, Spain and Portugal up to the level of the remainder of the EU and the level of expenditure that Germany found was necessary to unite East Germany with West Germany.

What about offsetting cost savings we can anticipate?

Well, let's start with the Border Patrol's annual budget of $7.8 billion. It stands to reason that if we removed the border with Mexico we could cut that budget in half and still have significantly improved security. There's $3.9 billion per year in savings.

The INS budget is roughly $6 billion. If we eliminate all of their work related to Mexican immigrants (both legal and illegal) that will surely have a major impact on their workload. If we also implemented the temporary reduction in legal immigration (excluding Mexico, of course, which would no longer be considered immigration per se), the lion's share of their work instantaneously evaporates. I would think that as a minimum we could cut their budget in half. That's another $3 billion in annual savings.

That leaves us with a net cost of about $8 billion per year, or $80 billion over 10 years.

More difficult to quantify and predict is the financial impact of a developed Mexico as an internal market within the United States. As a result of the German unification, the Western German economy went into a small boom. Western German GDP grew at a rate of 4.6 percent for 1990, reflecting the new demand from eastern Germany. The dramatic improvement in the western German figures resulted from the opening in eastern Germany of a large new market of 16 million persons and the simultaneous availability of many new workers from eastern Germany.[lxxii]

Ignoring this for the moment, where else might we get that $8 billion per year? Well, let's recall that every year taxpayers spend $225 billion dollars on tax preparation services. Let's do this: Switch to a simplified tax system such as a federal sales tax or a flat tax, and use some of the money people are currently paying to services like H&R Block to annex Mexico.

The specific numbers I'm proposing don't really matter much. Even if they're off by 100%, 200% or even 1,000% it still makes sense to annex Mexico into the U.S. and invest the money needed to bring those 100 million neighbors, friends, and consumers into the twenty-first century. The cost to date of the war in Iraq was about $350 billion as of this writing. Can anyone really maintain that if they compared spending $350 billion in Iraq versus spending $350 billion on Mexico we wouldn't get far more benefits—including security benefits—from spending the money on integrating Mexico into the United States?

Louisiana's U.S. senators Mary L. Landrieu and David Vitter introduced the Hurricane Katrina Disaster Relief and Economic Recovery Act, seeking $250 billion, or $500,000 per victim, to rebuild New Orleans. I'd rather give each victim $100,000 and tell them to settle down somewhere else because while there are still hurricanes, New Orleans will continue to be a disaster waiting to happen, particularly for the poor and indigent. We could then spend the rest to secure the southern third of this continent.

Still not convinced that we can come up with the money to make this work? Then let's put this issue to bed.

Pemex is the nationalized oil company in Mexico. Remember them, the folks who are losing money while sitting on two of the largest oil fields in the world. That's what happens when you nationalize industry, but that's not my point. We could *sell Pemex* to (carefully chosen) private concerns and use *that* money to pay for *everything!*

Still think it can't be accomplished?

The mind boggles...

Let's Get Some Balls!

What has stopped us from annexing Mexico isn't money, it isn't the Mexican army, and it isn't the Mexican people. It's the fact that we've become so afraid of what special interests will say that we won't admit the time has arrived for Mexico to become part of the United States. During the 1800s, the U.S. kept expanding and expanding, acquiring land in the Louisiana Purchase, the war with Mexico, the purchase of Alaska, and so on. It's probably the single most important factor that made us the powerful, and let's face it—rich nation that we are today. Were this not true, Americans would be sneaking across the border into Mexico instead of the other way around.

Let's summarize where we are:

The current situation is not working. We've got massive immigration, with countries from around the world (primarily Mexico) exporting their poverty problems to us, and the potential for terrorists capitalizing on this to the tune of a few million dead Americans in areas yet to be determined. It's costing us a fortune and destroying the environment in the process.

We can't effectively control our 2,000 mile-long southern border because we've got a Third World country with a caste system on the other side coupled with weak, fearful politicians and shortsighted business concerns.

The U.S. has a long history of expansion, and it's worked out very well for the people living in this country.

The majority of people in Mexico like the idea of becoming part of the United States assuming it would benefit them.

The government in Mexico has repeatedly shown that it can't (or won't) properly serve the people of Mexico. According to American notions of democracy and human rights, they have a right, in fact a duty, to replace it.

Investing the money needed to integrate Mexico into the United States and bring the people to a comparable standard of living with us would offer us huge benefits in areas as diverse as healthcare and security, and would open up a huge market that would benefit all concerned to a degree we may not yet be able to conceptualize.

The whole thing could be accomplished peacefully and there are numerous avenues available to pay for the enterprise.

So I say: Let's get half the balls of our ancestors, the ones who built the United States that we live in today. Let's make this happen *now!*

Appendix A
Chronology of U.S. Major Territorial Events

1783—Treaty with Britain marks first official boundary of the United States, with the Mississippi river as the western boundary and the top of Florida as the southern boundary.

1803—Louisiana Purchase roughly doubles the size of the United States.

1810—United States annexes Florida.

1812—United States attempts to annex Canada but fails.

1819—Spain formally gives up claim to Florida.

1821—Mexico gains independence from Spain.

1835—Texas rebels against Mexico.

1845—United States Annexes Texas

1846—United States sends troops to the Rio Grande, provoking a war with Mexico. United States Annexes Oregon Territory.

1848—United States flag flies over Mexico City. Treaty of Guadalupe Hidalgo is signed under which the U.S. annexes a territory the size of Western Europe, absorbing 100,000 Mexican citizens and 200,000 Native Americans in the process. All or part of the states of Texas, Arizona, New Mexico, Oklahoma, Wyoming, Colorado, Kansas, Utah, Nevada, and California became part of the US under the treaty.

1853—The Gadsden Treaty redefines the United States-Mexico boundary such that the United States gains additional land from Mexico, most notably the resource-rich areas of southern New Mexico.

1864—The first comprehensive federal immigration law, the Act to Encourage Immigration is designed to *increase* immigration so that US industries will have a sufficient labor supply during the Civil War.

1867—The United States purchases Alaska. Canada obtains independence from Britain.

1875—The law bars the immigration of convicts and of women for the purpose of prostitution, marking the first federal legislation restricting immigration into the United States.

1876—Congress declares void all state laws regulating immigration.

1882—The immigration Act of 1882 increases the restriction of immigrants, barring the entry of "idiots, lunatics, convicts, and persons likely to become public charges." The Chinese Exclusion Act bars the entry of Chinese laborers.

1891—The Immigration Act of 1891 orders the deportation of those who enter the United States without authorization and creates the Office of Immigration within the Department of the Treasury. The law also prohibits the admission of "polygamists, persons convicted of crimes involving moral turpitude, and those suffering a loathsome or contagious disease."

1893—US overthrows government of Hawaii.

1903—The Immigration Law of 1903 adds to the list of barred immigrants the categories of epileptics, the insane, professional beggars, and anarchists.

1907—The Act of February 20, 1907 requires that all boundary crossers enter the United States through an official port of entry.

1917—The Immigration Act of 1917 restates all past qualitative exclusions and also adds the categories of illiterates, requiring a literacy test and an eight-dollar head tax for entry. The legislation also establishes the "Asiatic Barred Zone," a geographic area that included most of Asia and the Pacific Islands, further restricting the entry of Asian immigrants.

1921—The Temporary Quota Act of 1921 limits the number of admissions of any one particular nationality to three percent of the group's population already in the United States according to the 1910 census.

1942—The Bracero Program begins.

1954—The INS launches Operation Wetback.

1959—Alaska and Hawaii become the 49th and 50th states.

1964—The Bracero Program ends.

1993—The U.S. Border Patrol launches Operation Blockade (later renamed Operation Hold-the-Line).

1994—The INS launches Operation Gatekeeper in San Diego. NAFTA goes into effect.

Appendix B
U.S. Border Patrol's
*Secure Border Initiative*lxxiii

The Secure Border Initiative (SBI) is a comprehensive multi-year plan to secure America's borders and reduce illegal migration. Homeland Security Secretary Michael Chertoff has announced an overall vision for the SBI which includes:

• More agents to patrol our borders, secure our ports of entry and enforce immigration laws;

• Expanded detention and removal capabilities to eliminate "catch and release" once and for all;

• A comprehensive and systemic upgrading of the technology used in controlling the border, including increased manned aerial assets, expanded use of UAVs, and next-generation detection technology;

• Increased investment in infrastructure improvements at the border—providing additional physical security to sharply reduce illegal border crossings; and

• Greatly increased interior enforcement of our immigration laws—including more robust worksite enforcement.

Staffing

Under SBI, our goal is to have operational control of both the northern and southern borders within five years.

• The President recently signed the Homeland Security Appropriations Bill into law, which included an 11% increase for U.S. Customs and Border Protection, bringing total funding to more than $7 billion—funds that will enable us to increase our physical presence at the border by hiring an additional 1,000 Border Patrol agents. With these new hires, Border Patrol will increase by nearly 3,000 agents since 9/11.

• The Homeland Security Appropriations Bill also includes roughly $3.9 billion in total funding for U.S. Immigration and Customs Enforcement (ICE) this fiscal year, a 9% increase over last year. Included are significant funding increases for ICE criminal investigators, detention beds, fugitive operations teams, and Immigration Enforcement agents.

• The increased funding will allow ICE to add roughly 250 new criminal investigators to better target the human smuggling organizations and other criminal groups that exploit our nation's borders. It will also allow ICE to add 400 new Immigration Enforcement Agents and 100 new Deportation Officers.

Detention and Removal

The vision for re-engineering the detention and removal process is to create an efficient system that will always have available detention capacity and a streamlined process to minimize the length of detention prior to removal of the alien.

• ***Detention Capacity:*** The Homeland Security Appropriations Bill contained funds that will enable us to add 2,000 new beds, bringing the total number of beds up to about 20,000. This action alone will allow us to remove thousands of illegal immigrants from our country. The Department of Homeland Security (DHS) is committed to developing innovative approaches to further expand our detention capacity, including exploring new partnerships with state and local governments.

109

• ***Expedited Removal (ER):*** DHS currently has the legislative authority to place certain classes of aliens into ER if they were apprehended nationwide within 2 years of entry. By policy, DHS has chosen to exercise this authority at all Ports of Entry and between Ports of Entry only along the Southwest border for aliens apprehended within 100 miles of the border and within 14 days of entry. DHS is reviewing options to expand ER further.

Technology and Infrastructure

DHS will field the most effective mix of current and next generation technology with appropriately trained personnel. Our goal is to ultimately have the capacity to integrate multiple state of the art systems and sensor arrays into a single comprehensive detection suite.

• ***Improved Technology:*** DHS will improve security in the areas between ports of entry by integrating and coordinating the use of technology including more Unmanned Aerial Vehicles (UAVs), aerial assets, Remote Video Surveillance camera systems, and sensors. DHS will create an integrated border security system, with awards beginning in fiscal year 2006 and deployment beginning in fiscal year 2007.

DHS obtained a Predator B UAV to enhance our ability to secure the southwest border, and we are taking opportunities to partner with the Department of Defense to utilize advanced but proven military technologies to help us with our border security mission.

• *Enhanced Infrastructure:* DHS will expand infrastructure systems throughout the border where appropriate to strengthen our efforts to reduce illegal entry to the United States-exemplified by Secretary Chertoff's announcement to waive certain legal requirements necessary to ensure expeditious completion of the 14-mile Border Infrastructure System near San Diego, California.

As in San Diego, DHS will improve border infrastructure in certain areas by increasing physical layers of security, building access roads to enable Border Patrol to speed response efforts, installing stadium style lighting to deter border crossers, and providing surveillance cameras to monitor incursion along targeted areas of the border.

Interior Enforcement

DHS will strengthen interior enforcement efforts to target those who enter illegally by unequivocally enforcing our laws and making sure that removal is achieved.

• ***Workplace Enforcement:*** DHS will implement an employer self-compliance program that will link government and business in a united effort to reduce the employment of unauthorized aliens in specific industries. The partnership will assemble a "best practices" methodology that employers will use to minimize certain known vulnerabilities in the legally required employment eligibility verification process. The employers will assist DHS by using their corporate and industry leadership to influence competitors, vendors, and contractors to adopt the best practices methods to ensure all businesses dealing with participating corporations are in compliance with legal hiring requirements.

DHS will seek to strengthen current worksite enforcement regulations to place an affirmative duty on employers to make inquiries on information suggesting that their employee is not authorized to work.

• **State and Local Partnerships**: DHS employs existing 287(g) authority to work with Corrections Departments of selected states, authorizing correctional officers to identify, process, and begin removal proceedings for incarcerated criminals before they are released. This facilitates their expeditious removal from the United States when their sentence ends. Currently, 287(g) programs have been established in Alabama, Florida, Arizona, and certain counties in California. DHS is also exploring the use of these partnerships as force multipliers in fugitive operations as well.

• **Criminal Alien Program (CAP):** CAP seeks to identify and remove all incarcerated criminal aliens from the United States. Key to this effort is identifying and screening foreign born aliens incarcerated in federal, state and major metropolitan jails and placing them into immigration proceedings prior to their release. The goal for CAP, with appropriate resources, is to screen 90% of all foreign born aliens in state and federal jails by FY09. Additionally, by FY10, a large percentage of aliens in major metropolitan jails will also be screened.

• **Fugitive Operations:** Currently, there are more than 450,000 absconders, and that number is growing at a rate of 40,000 per year. DHS will expand the national fugitive operations program so that in 10 years, DHS will eliminate the fugitive absconder population assuming appropriate resources. To achieve this goal will require the establishment of 100 fugitive operations teams nationwide (up from the current 44) as well as increased efficiencies in the program.

International Controls

Border-related crime affects communities on both sides of our land boundaries, and a shared approach is imperative to disrupting criminal groups and saving lives. SBI will be implemented in a way that entails an appropriate dialogue with the Governments of Mexico and Canada.

DHS will also work with other foreign governments to ensure they provide timely travel documents in order to remove the backlog of their nationals in our detention facilities. We will also ensure we maintain a productive dialogue in order to safely and quickly repatriate migrants back to their nations at the same rate at which they are arriving.

• **_Country Clearances:_** Working with the Department of State, DHS is in the

114

process of streamlining country clearances and internal U.S. government process changes that could cut several days from every escorted deportation.

• **Repatriation:** DHS has begun to aggressively examine this process with foreign governments to ensure better coordination with other nations in regard to our repatriation efforts. Often individuals who are removable remain in detention facilities because the foreign country has failed to provide a travel document in a timely fashion.

Appendix C
History of the INSlxxiv

"It's a big country; someone's got to furnish it."

Remember those ads for the Scandinavian furniture company IKEA? Our forefathers must have had similar thoughts, because during the nation's early years, Americans favored—indeed, encouraged—free, open immigration. It was a big country; they needed folks to settle it.

Not until the late 1800s did the public begin to question that policy. After the Civil War, some states started to pass their own immigration laws, which prompted the Supreme Court to rule in 1875 that immigration was a federal responsibility.

Immigration continued to rise in the 1880s, bringing an avalanche of cheap labor. With this influx of foreign cut-rate workers, economic conditions began to deteriorate in some areas, so Congress passed a series of immigration laws and fine-tuned the existing regulations. An increasingly complex web of laws and policies made it apparent that the nation needed a federal agency to enforce things from the top.

The Immigration Act of 1891 established an Office of the Superintendent of

Immigration within the Treasury Department. This office was responsible for admitting, rejecting, and processing all immigrants seeking admission to the United States and for implementing national immigration policy.

One of the office's first tasks was to collect arrival manifests—the lists of passengers from incoming ships. To do this, "immigrant inspectors," as they were called, were stationed at major American ports of entry.

U.S. Immigration Station, Angel Island, San Francisco, Calif., was billed as the "Ellis Island of the west." This early view shows the ship dock and passenger gangway leading to the main building.

118

The legendary immigration station at Ellis Island in New York opened in January 1892 and would remain the nation's largest, busiest station for decades to come. It teemed with immigrants and officials and representatives from the era's many immigrant-aid societies, who all worked in or passed through Ellis Island's hearing and detention rooms, hospitals, cafeterias, administrative offices, and railroad ticket offices. So massive were the goings-on at Ellis Island that by 1893 it employed 119 of the Superintendent's entire field and headquarters staff of 180.

The Superintendent of Immigration drew many of its early inspectors from state agencies or by hiring away former Customs and Chinese inspectors and by training recruits. The Immigration Act of 1882 had, among other provisions, a head tax of fifty cents on each immigrant. That money went into an "immigrant fund" that financed the fledgling immigration service until 1909, when Congress replaced the fund with an annual appropriation.

Legislation in March 1895 upgraded the Office of Immigration to the Bureau of Immigration and changed the agency head's title from Superintendent to Commissioner-General of Immigration.

The Bureau's first task was to formalize and standardize basic operating and regulatory procedures. For example, inspectors queried arrivals about their suitability for permanent entry and recorded their admission or rejection on manifest records. Detention guards cared for those who were detained until their cases were decided, or, if the decision was negative, until they were deported. Inspectors served on boards of special inquiry that reviewed each exclusion case.

The most frequent reason for exclusion was a foreigner's lack of money or nearby friends or relatives. The special inquiry board usually reversed that decision if someone could post bond for the immigrant or if one of the aid societies would take responsibility for him. Those to whom the board denied admission were deported at the expense of the transportation company that brought them to the United States port.

Main building of the U.S Immigration Station, Ellis Island, N.Y., circa 1900.

The head tax collected on immigrants in the Service's earliest years had placed the new agency within the Treasury Department. But in fact, Congress's primary interest in immigration, the reason it had become a federal concern in the first place, was to protect American workers and wages. This made immigration more a matter of commerce than revenue, so in 1903, Congress transferred the Bureau of Immigration to the newly created Department of Commerce and Labor.

There was another aspect to the matter of regulating immigration: The Constitution had assigned the task of naturalization, the process by which an immigrant becomes an American citizen, to Congress. Since 1802, however, Congress had been letting "any court of record" carry out this function. A century later, Congress appointed a commission to investigate how this haphazard approach to a serious national responsibility was working. In 1905, the commission reported—not surprisingly—that there was almost no uniformity in practices and procedures among the nation's more than 5,000 naturalization courts.

To address this lack of uniformity, Congress passed the Basic Naturalization Act of 1906, which established naturalization procedures that endure to this day. The Act encouraged state and local courts to relinquish their jurisdiction to federal courts, and it expanded the Bureau of Immigration into the Bureau of Immigration and Naturalization.

Immigration officers at the Immigration office located in the train depot at Portal, North Dakota, circa 1924.

Just seven years later, in 1913, the Department of Commerce and Labor reorganized into today's separate cabinet departments, and for a time, the Bureau of Immigration and Naturalization followed suit, each becoming a separate bureau, one for immigration, one for naturalization. They stayed like that until 1933.

Immigration from Europe decelerated quite a bit during World War I, but it resumed full-force after the war. Trying to control the influx, Congress instituted the national-origins quota system.

Laws passed in 1921 and 1924 limited the numbers of newcomers by assigning a quota to each nationality based upon its representation in previous U.S. census figures. Each year, the State Department issued a limited number of visas; only those immigrants who had obtained them and could present valid visas were permitted entry.

A corollary to severely restricted legal immigration is increased illegal immigration. So the quota-visa policy led to many of the immigration challenges that we see today.

Illegal entries and alien smuggling began to rise along land borders, so Congress created the Border Patrol, in 1924, within the Immigration Service. Stricter immigration policies coupled with Border Patrol apprehensions meant that agency staff and resources were becoming more heavily involved in deportations. And a corollary of deportations was that more aliens were conducting more court battles in order to stay.

U.S. Customs Inspectors and U.S. Immigration Inspectors process newly arrived Chinese immigrants on the railroad platform in Sumas, Wash., which served as the first Sumas border inspection station.

Thus was born the Immigration Board of Review, created within the Immigration Bureau in the mid-1920s. (The Board of Review became the Board of Immigration Appeals after moving to the Justice Department in the 1940s; it is now the Executive Office of Immigration Review.)

In 1933, the two agencies reunited by executive order into today's Immigration and Naturalization Service (INS).

With war brewing in Europe in the 1930s, immigration took on a new, prescient quality: not only was immigration a matter of economics, it was also becoming a matter of national security.

So President Roosevelt moved the INS from the Department of Labor to the Department of Justice in 1940. With this prophetic move, the task of securing our borders against enemy aliens was added to INS's wartime responsibilities. Its workforce doubled during the war years from approximately 4,000 to 8,000 employees.

National fears about the foreign-born continued to bubble up. In some instances, these fears were handled poorly, as when INS organized internment camps and detention facilities for enemy aliens, even when they were not actually enemies or aliens.

Immigration decreased after World War II. INS programs of the late 1940s and early '50s addressed the needs of returning GIs and the conditions in post-war Europe, restoring to America's immigration policies the heart that had temporarily been lost during the internment-camp era.

The War Brides Act of 1945 facilitated admission of the spouses and families of returning American soldiers. The Displaced Persons Act of 1948 and the Refugee Relief Act of 1953 allowed many refugees, displaced by the war and unable to enter the United States under regular immigration procedures, to be admitted. With the onset of the Cold War, the Hungarian Refugee Act of 1956, the Refugee-Escapee Act of 1957, and the Cuban Adjustment Program of the 1960s did much the same, offering a new home to the "huddled masses" who sought freedom, opportunity, and escape from tyranny.

The downside to America's open heart and outstretched arms was public concern—indeed, alarm—that our too-open post-war policies were letting criminal aliens, communists, subversives, and organized crime figures enter or remain in the United States along with legitimate refugees.

INS enforcement activities in the mid-1950s addressed those concerns. Public alarm over illegal aliens living and working in the United States resulted in stronger border controls and targeted deportation programs.

In 1965, Congress amended the body of immigration law by replacing the national-origins system with a preference system designed to reunite immigrant families and attract skilled workers. This change in national policy meant that the majority of applicants for immigration visas now came from Asia and Central and South America rather than Europe. Although the number of immigration visas available each year was still limited, Congress continued to pass special legislation, as it did for refugees from Indochina in the post-Vietnam era of the 1970s.

The Immigration Reform and Control Act of 1986 expanded the agency's responsibilities, making it more a modern-day law-enforcement agency. The Act charged INS with enforcing sanctions against American employers who hired undocumented aliens. This meant the INS was now investigating, prosecuting, and levying fines against corporate and individual employers and deporting aliens found to be working here illegally. But this same law allowed certain illegal aliens, in certain circumstances, to legalize their residence here, and INS also administered that program.

As travel and technology helped make the world a smaller place, the emphasis on controlling illegal immigration for all the reasons discussed above—economic, national-security, crime-control—fostered INS's growth in the late twentieth century. The workforce that had numbered some 8,000 from World War II through the late 1970s grew to more than 30,000 employees in 36 districts around the world by 1998.

The one-time force of immigrant inspectors became a corps of officers specializing in inspection, examination, adjudication, legalization, investigation, patrol, and refugee and asylum issues. These very skills and specialties made for a natural marriage with the U.S. Customs Service after 9/11. Legacy INS employees now work in one of three agencies—the Bureau of Citizenship and Immigration Service, the Bureau of Immigration and Customs Enforcement, and the Bureau of Customs and Border Protection.

Today's Bureau of Customs and Border Protection provides for selective immigration and controlled entry of tourists, business travelers, other temporary visitors, as well as all kinds of merchandise and commodities for private and commercial purposes—every animal, mineral, or vegetable that crosses our borders, no matter the reason.

Appendix D
The Threat of
Nuclear Smuggling.^{lxxv}

The Customs and Border Protection currently employs a multi-layered approach to protect America from the introduction of nuclear weapons, radiation dispersal bombs (dirty bombs), and other Weapons of Mass Destruction (WMD).

• As a first line of defense, CBP works to prevent adversaries from illegally obtaining sensitive U.S. technology and components that they may need to assemble a WMD.

• Second, CBP trains and equips foreign authorities to interdict smuggled WMD materials at their own borders, before such materials fall into hostile hands or arrive in America.

• Third, CBP has launched major initiatives to prevent the global trading system from being exploited by terrorists to introduce WMD into this country.

• Finally, CBP uses a variety of systems at America's border, the last line of defense, to ensure that nuclear materials and other WMD do not enter this country.

1. Keeping Nuclear Components Out of the Hands of Adversaries—History and Enforcement

Project Shield America—U.S. adversaries frequently seek to illegally obtain sensitive technology and equipment from America for use in developing WMD and other weapons systems. For more than 20 years, CBP has served as the lead agency for enforcing U.S. export control laws to prevent such schemes. CBP relies on strategic investigations, intelligence, and outbound exams to prevent these materials from being illegally exported. In Dec. 2001, CBP enhanced its export enforcement through a program called Project Shield America, which seeks to keep sensitive U.S. weapons components out of the hands of terrorists. As part of the program, CBP has identified key U.S. weapons components that may be sought by terrorists. CBP is partnering with U.S. manufacturers of these items to guard against illegal foreign acquisition. Since Dec. 2001, CBP agents have visited nearly 3,000 U.S. firms to solidify this partnership. These visits have also spawned numerous criminal probes. Over the years, CBP strategic investigations

130

have targeted hundreds of illegal weapons export schemes. Some of the most serious:

• *Nuclear Trigger Devices Bound for Israel*—In April 2002, Richard Smyth, a former NATO advisor and president of Milco International, was sentenced for exporting nuclear trigger devices to Israel. Smyth had been charged in 1985 with exporting 800 devices known as krytrons to Israel without obtaining the required export license. Krytrons have civilian and military uses, but are considered ideal for triggering nuclear weapons. Before trial, Smyth fled. After 16 years on the run, Smyth was arrested in Spain in July 2001 and extradited to Los Angeles where he pleaded guilty to two counts in the original 1985 indictment.

• *Nuclear-Grade Zirconium Bound for Iraq*—In June 1995, CBP agents in New York arrested three men on charges of attempting to smuggle seven tons of nuclear-grade zirconium to Iraq. The investigation, in which undercover CBP agents posed as Iraqi military officials, resulted in the seizure of five tons of zirconium in America and another two tons in Cyprus. Zirconium is a material used to cover nuclear fuel in a reactor core. The zirconium in this case had been smuggled from Ukraine, through

131

Germany, to New York and Cyprus, where it awaited export to Iraq.

• *Nuclear Trigger Devices Bound for Iraq*—In March 1990, CBP agents working with British authorities intercepted 40 nuclear trigger devices in London that were destined for Iraq. The 18-month undercover probe by Customs and Border Protection established that the shipment of krytrons, falsely labeled as "air conditioning parts," had been ordered from America by an Iraqi front company in England called Euromac. Several Iraqi agents were arrested in England in connection with the case.

• *Sarin Nerve Gas Bound for Iran* -- In May 1989, Juwhan Yun, the president of a New Jersey firm called Komex International, was convicted of conspiring to export 500 units of sarin nerve gas to Iran. The conviction resulted from an undercover CBP investigation in which agents learned that the defendant was working with a London arms broker whose Iranian clients sought sarin gas to be dropped from aircraft in Mark 94 bombs. The London arms broker, Charles Caplan, remains a fugitive.

2. Interdicting Nuclear Materials Overseas and International Counter-Proliferation Training

Since the early 1990s, Customs and Border Protection has provided non-proliferation training and equipment to nearly 3,000 border guards and CBP officials in 26 nations to counter the spread of WMD and their components. With funding by the U.S. State and Defense Departments, CBP administers this training to nations in Eastern Europe, Central Asia, the Caucuses, the Middle East, and Asia. CBP also maintains permanent advisors in many of these nations to facilitate local training and equipment delivery. The goal is to help these nations interdict WMD materials being smuggled across their borders before they fall into hostile hands or arrive in America.

CBP delivers WMD training to foreign authorities both in-country and in America. One of the most important courses offered is "RADACAD" or Radiation Academy training at the Department of Energy's Pacific Northwest National Laboratory in Washington State. This is the only program in the world where authorities can train with actual nuclear materials in smuggling scenarios. CBP also provides courses ranging from tracker training to detect WMD smuggling between ports of entry to training in advanced undercover operations.

CBP also delivers millions of dollars worth of high-tech and low-tech detection equipment to foreign authorities to meet the counter-proliferation needs of each nation. CBP has delivered roughly 600 personal radiation detectors (or radiation pagers) to foreign authorities, as well as X-ray vans equipped with radiation detectors, and gamma ray inspection systems. CBP has also provided low-tech items, such as fiber-optic scopes, drills, mirrors, and tools used to search vehicles at borders.

Customs and Border Protection WMD counter-proliferation programs have achieved encouraging results. Since 1998, there have been at least eight significant seizures by foreign authorities that have been attributed to Customs and Border Protection training and/or equipment, including the following:

• **Weapons-Grade Uranium Seized in Bulgaria**—In May 1999, Bulgarian customs officials at the Ruse border crossing in Bulgaria discovered 10 grams of highly enriched uranium (U-235) inside a lead "pig" concealed in an air compressor in the trunk of a car. The 35-year-old Turkish driver was transporting his nuclear cargo from Turkey to Moldova. It is believed the smuggler was offering this small shipment of U-235 as a "sample" to buyers in Moldova in advance of a larger shipment of the same materials. The Bulgarian customs officer who found the U-235 had just received counter-proliferation training from Customs and Border Protection. His supervisor had been trained by Customs and Border Protection at RADACAD. The Bulgarian lab director who examined and identified the materials had also received training from CBP and Border Protection.

• **Radioactive Lead Containers Seized in Uzbekistan**—In March 2000, Uzbekistan customs officials at the Gisht Kuprink border crossing discovered 10 highly radioactive lead containers concealed in 23 tons of scrap stainless steel in a truck entering from Kazakhstan. Documents found in the truck indicated that the Iranian driver was planning to deliver his radioactive cargo to Quetta, Pakistan, near the border of Afghanistan. Uzbeki authorities found the radioactive material after their radiation pagers alerted as the truck entered the customs post. The radiation pagers that alerted to the truck had been provided to Uzbeki authorities by Customs and Border Protection in May 1999. The Uzbeki authorities had also been provided with extensive WMD non-proliferation training by Customs and Border Protection.

3. Keeping Nuclear Materials Out of the Global Trading System

a. Container Security Initiative—In Jan. 2002, U.S. Customs launched the Container Security Initiative (CSI), an initiative to prevent global containerized cargo from being exploited by terrorists to inflict harm on America and other nations. The initiative is designed to enhance security of the sea cargo container—a vital link in global trade. Some 200 million sea cargo containers move annually among the world's top seaports, and nearly 50 percent of the value of all U.S. imports arrive via sea containers.

One of the core elements of CSI involves placing CBP inspectors at major foreign seaports to pre-screen cargo containers before they are shipped to America. Customs and Border Protection is negotiating with foreign authorities in Europe, Asia, and other locations to place CBP inspectors at some of the world's largest seaports. CBP officials, working with their foreign counterparts, would be in a position to detect potential nuclear materials or WMD in U.S.-bound containers at these foreign ports. Since roughly half of all sea containers that enter the United States pass through 10 major seaports around the globe, CBP is initially focusing on these ports as key "chokepoints" in the global trading system.

• *CBP Inspectors Placed at Select Canadian Seaports*—Customs and Border Protection has already put inspectors at three Canadian seaports through an agreement reached with Canadian Customs. In March 2002, teams of CBP inspectors were placed in Montreal, Halifax, and Vancouver to pre-screen cargo that is offloaded at these ports and destined for America. At the same time, Canadian Customs has placed its own inspectors at the U.S. seaports of Newark and Seattle to pre-screen cargo bound for Canada. The agreement with Canada is expected to be the first of many similar agreements around the globe.

As part of the CSI, CBP is also working with foreign nations to establish basic criteria for authorities to use in identifying high-risk containers. CBP is also working on the deployment of detection technology to foreign ports help screen containers. Finally, CBP is researching and testing new technology, such as tamper-proof seals, to make containers themselves more secure against terrorist exploitation.

b. Customs and Border Protection Trade Partnership Against Terrorism

In April 2002, Customs and Border Protection unveiled an industry partnership program that enlists importers, carriers, and manufacturers to secure every aspect of the international supply chain against the terrorist threat—from the foreign loading dock, to the cargo conveyance, to the port of entry in America. Called the CBP Trade Partnership Against Terrorism or CTPAT, the initiative offers those companies that improve the security of their supply chains expedited processing through Customs and Border Protection. The goal is to enhance the security of cargo entering the U.S. while improving the flow of trade. More than 60 companies, including General Motors, Ford Motor Co., Motorola, Inc, and DaimlerChrysler A.G., have signed up to participate and 100 more firms have applications pending.

Businesses that participate in CTPAT are required to conduct a comprehensive self-assessment of their supply chain security and submit a security questionnaire to CBP. They must also develop and implement a long-term program to enhance their supply chain security and communicate CTPAT guidelines to other companies that they work with in the supply chain. For companies that take these steps, CBP will provide expedited processing of their goods and conveyances at U.S. borders. CBP may offer participants dedicated commercial lanes and reduced inspections.

4. Stopping Nuclear Materials at U.S. Borders

a. **Risk Targeting and Intelligence—** Contrary to media reports that CBP only pays attention to two percent of sea cargo entering America, CBP actually employs a multi-layered process that scrutinizes virtually all incoming sea cargo and targets those shipments that pose the highest risk. CBP receives electronic information on more than 95 percent of all U.S.-bound sea cargo before it arrives in this country. This data includes manifest information on the type of commodity, the manufacturer, the shipper, the consignee, the country of origin, the routing, and the terms of payment. CBP uses vast computer systems to sort through this data and assign a numeric score to each shipment indicating its level of risk. Special CBP teams called Manifest Review Units also scrutinize manifest and bill of lading data for each incoming shipment. These units have access to a vast array of databases, including intelligence data, to help them conduct analysis. Based upon rules-based criteria and the analysis of the Manifest Review Units, containers that are determined to pose a potential security risk (high-risk containers) are flagged to receive a security inspection upon arrival using detection technology. This entire process takes place before the cargo arrives.

b. Detection Technology—At the nation's ports of entry, CBP employs a wide range of technology to examine incoming shipments that are high-risk. Many of these technological devices are designed specifically to detect nuclear/radioactive materials. For example, CBP currently has more than 4,000 personal radiation pagers deployed around the country. By next January, this number will more than double to 8,500 radiation pagers nationwide. At many ports, CBP is also installing portal radiation detectors, which are fixed devices that can detect various types of radiation. In addition, CBP is deploying isotope identifiers that allow inspectors to determine whether a source of radiation is a possible terrorist threat or a commercial / medical source of radiation. CBP is also exploring the use of crane-mounted radiation detection devices to detect radioactive materials in sea cargo containers.

CBP also maintains an arsenal of non-intrusive technology that allows inspectors to detect hidden compartments and other anomalies in goods and conveyances entering the country. Gamma-ray imaging systems, known as Vehicle And Cargo Inspection Systems (VACIS), are deployed at major ports of entry. CBP also employs hundreds of X-ray systems at ports around the country, some of which are equipped with radiation detection equipment. Other detection technology in use includes density measuring devices, fiber-optic scopes, acoustic inspection systems, and low-tech tools.

c. Physical Inspections—CBP inspectors conducting physical examinations on the front lines form the most important factor in keeping nuclear materials and other contraband from entering America. Using their training, intuition, and experience to detect anomalies and inconsistencies, these officers are the linchpins of the inspection process. In 1999, the training and intuition of a single CBP inspector was the key to preventing an Al Qaeda terrorist from blowing up a major U.S. airport:

• *Millennium Bomber Intercepted*—On Dec. 14, 1999, an Algerian man named Ahmed Ressam arrived at the tiny U.S.

141

Customs port of entry in Port Angeles, Washington, after taking a ferry from Victoria, Canada. Ressam was the last to drive off the ferry in his rental car. A Customs inspector approached the vehicle and began questioning Ressam. With no advanced warning about this individual or detection technology to help her screen his vehicle, the inspector simply relied on her training and intuition to determine that this traveler posed a serious risk. The inspector noted that Ressam had taken an odd travel route and appeared nervous and uncooperative. Suspicions raised, the inspector asked Ressam to step out of the car for a trunk search. After exiting the vehicle, Ressam fled on foot. Customs inspectors chased him down and arrested him. In the trunk of the car, inspectors found nitroglycerine, timing devices, circuit boards, and more than 100 pounds of bomb making materials. Ressam was later convicted of conspiracy to bomb Los Angeles International Airport with these materials. It was later determined that he had been trained by Al Qaeda in Afghanistan to carry out attacks on America.

Since September 11, CBP inspectors at all the nation's ports of entry have been on Alert Level One. Under this level of alert, CBP inspectors conduct dramatically enhanced inspections of cargo and conveyances entering the country. In recent months, Customs and Border Protection has also increased its counter-terrorism training for officers on the front lines. Inspectors are being given specific instruction in identifying WMD materials, their concealment methods, and how to respond to WMD incidents. Some CBP inspectors are also being trained with "live" nuclear materials in smuggling exercises at RADACAD or the Radiation Academy at the Department of Energy's Pacific Northwest National Laboratory. Tabletop and field exercises involving WMD smuggling are also part of the counter-terrorism training for CBP inspectors.

Appendix E
Guide for the Mexican Migrant[lxxvi]

Distributed by the Mexican Ministry of Foreign Relations

INTRODUCTION

Esteemed Countryman:
The purpose of this guide is to provide you with practical advice that may prove useful to you in case you have made the difficult decision to search for employment opportunities outside of your country.

The sure way to enter another country is by getting your passport from the Ministry of Foreign Affairs, and the visa, which you may apply for at the embassy or consulate of the country you wish to travel to.

However, in practice we see many Mexicans who try to cross the Northern Border without the necessary documents, through high-risk zones that involve grave dangers, particularly in desert areas or rivers with strong, and not always obvious, currents.

Reading this guide will make you aware of some basic questions about the legal consequences of your stay in the United States of America without the appropriate migratory documents, as well as about the rights you have in that country, once you are there, independent of your migratory status.

Keep in mind always that there exist legal mechanisms to enter the United States of America legally.

In any case, if you encounter problems or run into difficulties, remember that Mexico has 45 consulates in that country whose locations you can find listed in this publication.

Familiarize yourself with the closest consulate and make use of it.

DANGERS IN CROSSING HIGH RISK ZONES

To cross the river can be very risky, above all if you cross alone and at night.

Heavy clothing increases in weight when wet and this makes swimming and floating difficult.

If you cross by desert, try to walk at times when the heat will not be too intense.

Highways and population centers are far apart, which means you will spend several days looking for roads, and you will not be able to carry foodstuffs or water for long periods of time. Also, you can get lost.

Salt water helps keep liquids in your body. Although you may feel more thirst if you drink salt water, the risk of dehydration is much less.

The symptoms of dehydration are:

—Little or no sweat.

—Dryness in the eyes and in the mouth.

—Headache.

—Tiredness and excessive exhaustion.

—Difficulty in walking and thinking.

—Hallucinations and visions.

If you get lost, guide yourself by light posts, train tracks, or dirt roads.

BEWARE OF HUMAN TRAFFICKERS (COYOTES, POLLEROS)

They can deceive you with assurances of crossing in a few hours through the mountains and deserts. This is simply not so!

They can risk your life taking you across rivers, drainage canals, desert areas, train tracks, or highways. This has caused the death of hundreds of persons.

If you decide to hire people traffickers to cross the border, consider the following precautions:

Do not let them out of your sight. Remember that they are the only ones who know the lay of the land, and therefore the only ones who can get you out of that place.

Do not trust those who offer to take you to "the other side" and ask you to drive a car or to take or carry a package for them. Normally, those packages contain drugs or other prohibited substances. For this reason, many people have ended up in jail.

If you transport other persons, you can be confused with a human trafficker, and they can accuse you of the crime of trafficking or auto theft.

Do not entrust your minor children to strangers who offer to take them across to the United States.

151

DO NOT USE FALSE DOCUMENTS
DO NOT USE FALSE DOCUMENTS OR THOSE THAT DO NOT BELONG TO YOU, NOR DECLARE A FALSE NATIONALITY.

If you try to cross with false documents or those of another person, take into account the following:

To use false documents or those of another person is a federal crime in the United States, for which you can be tried in a criminal proceeding and end up in jail; likewise, if you use a false name or say that you are a citizen of the United States when you are not one.

Do not lie to officials of the United States at ports and points of entry.

IF YOU ARE ARRESTED

Do not resist arrest.

Do not assault or insult officials.

Do not throw rocks or objects at officials or at patrols since this is considered a provocation by those officials.

If they believe themselves to be under attack, it is likely that they will use force to arrest you.

Raise your hands slowly so that they see you are not armed.

Do   not

have in your hands any object that could be considered a weapon such as spotlights, screwdrivers, pocketknives, knives, or rocks.

Do not run or try to escape.

Do not hide in dangerous places.

Do not cross high-speed highways.

It is better to be arrested for a few hours and repatriated to Mexico than to get lost in the desert.

IF THEY ARREST YOU, YOU HAVE RIGHTS!

Give your real name.

If you are a minor accompanied by an adult, tell the authorities so they do not separate you.

Your rights are:

To know where you are.

To ask that they allow you to contact a representative of the closest Mexican consulate for assistance.

Not to make statements or to sign documents, above all if they are in English, without the advice of a defense lawyer or Mexican consular representative.

To receive medical attention if you are injured or in delicate health.

To be respected in your person and to receive dignified treatment without regard to your migratory status.

To have safe transport.

155

To have food and water whenever you need it.

You are not obligated to state your migratory status at the time of arrest.

You have the right not to be beaten or insulted.

Not to be held incomunicado.

In case they take away your things, ask for a receipt so that you can claim them upon release.

It is important that you inform your lawyer or Mexican consular representative who visits you of any infringement of these rights. Also, inform the closest office of the Ministry of Foreign Affairs in Mexico.

If you want more information and you live in Texas or the city of Acuña, Coahuila, tune in to "La Poderosa" (The Powerful) at 1570 AM.

IN CASE OF ARREST

If you are sentenced for a crime or you are jailed and facing a criminal proceeding, you have the following rights:

Not to be discriminated against by the police, the courts, or prison officials.

To receive visits by Mexican consular personnel and members of your family.

To receive legal representation without conditions and obstacles.

157

If you are facing a criminal proceeding and you have not yet been sentenced, ask your lawyer or consular representative about pleading guilty.

"Laws."

Do not declare yourself guilty without first consulting your lawyer about the chances of winning your case.

It is important that you know the laws of the state where you live and work since the laws in each one are different. Consider the following advice:

If you drink, do not drive, since if you do not have documents, you can be arrested and deported.

If a legal resident is convicted more than twice for drinking under the influence, he can be deported.

Do not drive without a driver's license.

Respect traffic laws and use your seatbelt.

Do not drive without insurance and do not agree to drive a stranger's car.

Do not let strangers into your car.

If when driving, you commit a traffic infraction and you are stopped by the police, place your hands on the steering wheel and do not get out of the car until the officer requests that you do so.

Avoid calling attention to yourself while you normalize your stay or process your documents to live in the United States.

The best way is not to change your routine of going from your job to your home.

Avoid noisy parties. The neighbors can get annoyed and call the police, and you can be arrested.

Avoid getting involved in fights.

If you go to a bar or nightclub, and a fight starts, leave, since in the confusion you could be arrested even though you have not done anything.

Avoid family or domestic violence. As in Mexico, it is a crime in the United States.

Domestic violence is not only physical, but it also includes threats, screaming, and ill-treatment.

If you are accused of domestic violence against your children, spouse, or some other person who lives with you, you could go to jail. In addition, the Child Protective Service could take away your children.

Do not carry firearms, knives, or other dangerous objects. Keep in mind that many Mexicans are dead or in prison for that.

If the police enter your house or apartment, do not resist. However, ask for a proper warrant. It is better to cooperate and to seek to communicate with the closest Mexican consulate.

"Search Warrant."

CONSULATES

The Ministry of Foreign Affairs has 45 consular offices in the Interior and on the Southern Border of the United States of America whose function is to help you. Remember, if you have been arrested or are serving a prison term, you have the right to communicate with the closest Mexican Consulate.

Always carry your Consular Protection Guide. Stay close to the Consulate. Stay close to

161

Mexico.
It is your home, Countryman!

MINISTRY OF FOREIGN AFFAIRS General Directorate of Protection and Consular Affairs

MEXICAN CONSULATES IN THE UNITED STATES

Albuquerque
Tel. (5C5) 247-21-47
Austin
Tel. (512) 478-23-00
Brownsville
Tel. (956) 542-44-31
Chicago
Tel. (312) 738-23-83
Del Río
Tel. (830) 775-23-52
Detroit
Tel. (313) 964-45-15
Eagle Pass
Tel. (830) 773-92-55
Filadelfia
Tel. (215) 922-42-62
Houston
Tel. (713) 271-68-00
Kansas
Tel. (816) 556-08-00
Las Vegas
Tel. (7C2) 383-06-23

Atlanta
Tel. (404)266-22-33
Boston
Tel. (617) 426-41-81
Colexico
Tel. (760) 357-38-63
Dallas
Tel. (214) 252-92-50
Denver
Tel. (303) 331-11-10
Douglas
Tel. (520) 364-31-07/42
El Paso
Tel. (915) 533-85-55
Fresno
Tel. (559) 233-30-65
Indianápolis
Tel. (317)951-00-05
Laredo
Tel. (956) 723-63-69
Los Ángeles
Tel. (213) 351-68-00

CONSULADOS		ESTADOS

Mc Allen
Tel. (956) 686-02-43
Nogales
Tel. (520) 287-25-21
Omaha
Tel. (402) 595-18-41
Oxnard
Tel. (805) 984-87-38
Portland
Tel. (503) 274-14-42
Raleigh
Tel. (919) 754-00-46
Salt Lake City
Tel. (801) 521-85-02
San Bernardino
Tel. (909) 889-98-36
San Francisco
Tel. (415) 354-17-00
Santa Ana
Tel. (714) 835-30-69
Tucson
Tel. (520) 882-55-95
Yuma
Tel. (928) 343-00-66

Miami
Tel. (786) 268-49-00
Nueva York
Tel. (212) 217-64-00
Orlando
Tel. (407) 422-05-14
Phoenix
Tel. (602) 242-73-98
Presidio
Tel. (915) 229-27-88
Sacramento
Tel. (916) 441-32-87
San Antonio
Tel. (210) 227-10-85/86
San Diego
Tel. (619) 231-84-14
San José
Tel. (408) 294-34-14
Seattle
Tel. (206) 448-35-26
Washington
Tel. (202) 736-10-00

STATE GOVERNMENTS
DIRECTORY OF OFFICES IN THE MEXICAN
REPUBLIC CONCERNED WITH MIGRANTS

Aguascalientes (449) 918-76-45
Baja California 01-68-65-58-10-57
Baja California Sur 01-612-12-29-008
Campeche 01-981-811-9217/16/15
Chiapas (55) 5207-4260
Chihuahua (614) 429-33-00
Coahuila (884) 412-46-49
Colima (312) 330-30-16

Distrito Federal (55) 5341-1483
Durango (618) 811-41-36
Nuevo León 01-81-20-20-31-16/17
Oaxaca (951) 513-13-11
Edo. de México (55) 5540-5590
Guanajuato (473) 734-0272 al 74
Puebla (222) 242-52-46
Querétaro (442) 238-50-00 Ext. 5891
Guerrero (747) 472-79-94
Hidalgo 01800 717-0828 (771) 717-60-52
Quintana Roo 01-800-716-22-44 01-983-83-505-00 Ext. 1179/1211
San Luis Potosí (444) 812-98-19
Jalisco (333) 668-18-01
Michoacán (443) 317-83-01 y 02
Sinaloa (667) 714-22-97
Sonora (662) 213-46-13
Morelos (777) 317-05-25
Nayarit (311) 217-28-09
Tabasco 01-993-314-36-71
Tamaulipas (834) 312-92-39

163

Tlaxcala
(246) 461-03-29

 Veracruz
(228) 812-26-46/0738

 Yucatán
01800-010-68-6292
(999) 928-72-67
Ext. 26017

 Zacatecas
(492) 923-95-98

This Consular Protection Guide does not promote crossing by Mexicans without the legal documentation required by the government of the United States. Its purpose is to make known the risks, and to inform the migrants about their rights, whether they are legal residents or not.

Appendix F
Immigration's Impact on the
U.S.

Immigrant Admissions (INS 1996-2005): **8,737,612**
Illegal Alien Population (2005 FAIR est.): **10,853,000**
Projected Population - 2025 (2001 FAIR): **393,883,000**

IMMIGRATION IS A NATIONAL ISSUE

Americans now realize that the costs of our present high level of immigration (legal and illegal) are enormous and growing. (The Center for Immigration Studies estimated in 1995 that immigration costs us a net $29 billion a year –more than the combined budgets of the Departments of State, Justice and Interior.) These costs include both programs targeted toward immigrants, as well as the increased costs of education, health care, and welfare programs that are used by immigrants.

Much of the news coverage of this problem focuses solely on the six states with the highest immigration levels: California, New York, Texas, Florida, New Jersey and Ilinois. But do not be misled: High immigration is not a problem just for these six states; it is a problem for the entire country.

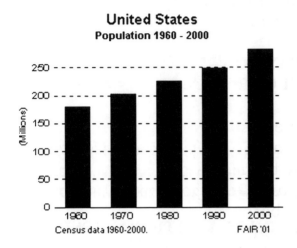

United States
Population 1960 - 2000

Census data 1960-2000.   FAIR '01

EVERY STATE RECEIVES IMMIGRANTS AND FEELS THE IMPACT

Every state receives immigration. Mississippi, for example, is not known as a "high-impact" state. Yet it has the nation's fastest growing immigrant population (up by 476% since 1990—from less than 1% of its population then to about 4.3% now). Other states that are newly experiencing large-scale immigrant settlement include Colorado (up 136%), North Carolina (up 129%), Oregon (up 115%), Nebraska (up 107%) and Utah (up 102%).

Consider Hawaii. Although it receives fewer immigrants than, say, Florida, it still takes more than its fair share. In Hawaii, nine percent of the population consists of immigrants who arrived since 1980; by way of comparison, six percent of Florida's population consists of recent immigrants.

WE ALL PAY FOR IMMIGRATION THROUGH OUR FEDERAL TAXES

Much of the cost for immigration is paid by the states and municipalities, but a lot is paid for by the federal government too. Illegal immigrants receive taxpayer support for their U.S.-born children, immunizations, subsidized public health and other programs. Legal immigrants are eligible for almost all federal programs. In many areas, such as education, the federal government gives matching grants for state expenditures, which means paying twice for those costs of immigration. When states hand a bill to the federal government for the costs of immigration (as is provided for by law in the case of incarceration of illegal immigrants, or welfare programs for the illegal aliens who were "amnestied" in 1986), it is you who will pay regardless of where you live.

The U.S. is a vast country; it is easy to be deceived into thinking that what goes on in other states does not affect us. But, directly or indirectly, the impact of high immigration on our country hits us all and hits us hard. For that reason, all Americans should demand that their representatives in Washington reduce the price they are paying for immigration. The best way to cut those costs is to reduce immigration itself.

NATIONAL POPULATION

Between 1990 and 2000 the U.S. population increased by 13.1 percent (from 248,909,873 to 281,421,906). This was 1.4 million more people than were expected, which Census Bureau officials said may have been because a better job was done in counting illegal aliens than in the past.

The population increase over the decade of the 1990s was due to a 57.4 percent increase in the foreign-born population and a 9.2 percent increase in the native-born population (including children born to the immigrants). Overall, the increase in the immigrant population directly accounted for 34.9 percent of the nation's rise in population.

Between 1980 and 1990 the U.S. population increased by 9.9 percent (from 226,542,203 to 248,909,873 residents).

FOREIGN-BORN POPULATION

FAIR estimates that the U.S. foreign-born population was about 36,819,700 residents in July 2005. This meant a foreign-born population share of 12.4 percent. The amount of change since the 2000 Census indicates an average annual rate of increase in the foreign-born population of about 1,142,425 people, which is 40.4 percent of the nation's annual average population increase. In addition, the Center for Immigration Studies recently estimated that 23 percent of babies being born in the United States are to foreign-born mothers. This share of current births would be about 4,905,855 children born to immigrants in 2004-05, and the total share of population increase combining new immigration and births to foreign-born mothers would be about 73 percent of the nation's overall population increase.

The 2000 Census recorded 31,107,573 foreign-born residents in the country. That was 11.1 percent of the country's overall population and an increase of 57.4 percent above the 1990 foreign-born population of 19,767,316 residents. The numerical increase in the foreign-born population between 1990-2000 was 11.3 million, which demonstrates that the average increase over that period has been more than one million per year.

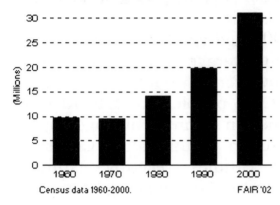

United States
Foreign-Born Population 1960-2000

Census data 1960-2000.   FAIR '02

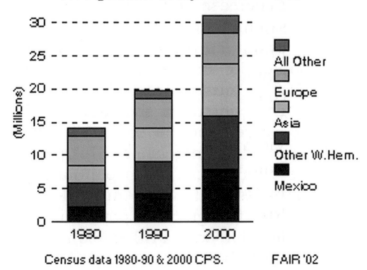

United States
Foreign-Born Composition 1980-00

Census data 1980-90 & 2000 CPS.   FAIR '02

The more than 50 percent surge in the immigrant population was much higher than the 9.3 percent increase in the native-born population. This is why the foreign-born population share increased from 9.7 percent to 11.1 percent.

The 2000 Census recorded that 13,178,276 of the country's foreign-born residents had entered the country during the previous ten years - an average of 1.3 million increase per year. This constituted 42.4 percent of the foreign-born population.

Speakers of Foreign Languages
(at home in the United States in the 2000 Census)

Spanish	28,100,725
French	1,606,790
Chinese	1,499,635
German	1,382,615
Tagalog	1,224,240
Vietnamese	1,009,625
Italian	1,008,370
Korean	894,065
Russian	706,240
Polish	667,415
Arabic	614,580
Portuguese	563,835

(Source: Census Bu-
reau report: Language
Spoken at Home for
the Population 5 Years
and Over, April 2004)

An indicator of the change the country
is experiencing as a result of mass immigration may be seen in 2000 Census data
on language spoken at home. The data
show that compared to the 1990 Census
finding that 13.8 percent of the population
over 5-years old spoke a language other
than English at home, in 2000 that share
had risen to 17.6 percent. Among the non-
English speakers at home, those who
spoke Spanish rose from 54.5 percent in
1990 to 59.6 percent in 2000. Less than
half (45.4%) of those who said they spoke a
language other than English at home in
2000 also said they spoke English less
than very well.

* 2000 Census data for China include
Hong Kong and Taiwan;
Data for Soviet Union include Russia,
Ukraine & Belarus.

The twelve countries above constituted three-fifths (60.7%) of the foreign-
born population in 2000. Mexico alone accounted for more than one-quarter (29.5%)
of the foreign-born total. Compared to the

4,443,601 Mexican-born residents from the 2000 Census who said they entered the United States between 1990-2000, INS data (see below) indicate that the total number of legal Mexican immigrants during that period numbered about 1,133,300 persons.

Foreign-Born Change Since 1980: Top Ten Countries 1980-2000 (in thousands)

Rank	Country	1980	Country	1990	Country	2000
1	Mexico	2,199	Mexico	4,298	Mexico	9,177
2	Germany	849	Philip.	913	China *	1,519
3	Canada	843	Canada	745	Philip.	1,369
4	Italy	832	Cuba	737	India	1,023
5	U.K	669	Germany	712	Vietnam	988
6	Cuba	608	U.K	640	Cuba	873
7	Philip.	501	Italy	581	Korea	864
8	Poland	418	Korea	568	Canada	821
9	Sov.Un.	406	Vietnam	543	El Sal.	817
10	Korea	290	China	530	Germany	707
11	China	286	El Sal.	465	Dom.Rep.	688
12	Vietnam	231	India	450	U.K.	678
	All Others	5,949	All Other	8,585	All Others	12,238
	Total	14,080	Total	19,767	Total	31,108

Findings by the Center for Immigration Studies from the Census Bureau's 2000 Current Population Survey (CPS) were:

• 17.6 percent of all children four-years old and younger were born to immigrant mothers. A comparable share (16.3%) of older children were also born to immigrant mothers.

• 40.1 percent of immigrants aged 18 and older have become U.S. citizens.

• 44 percent of immigrants and their children are in poverty or near poverty (compared to 27.8% of native-born residents).

• 30.9 percent of immigrants and their children do not have health insurance (compared with 13% of native-born residents).

• 19.7 percent of immigrant-headed households receive welfare—despite the fact that illegal immigrants are ineligible for welfare—(compared with 13.3% of native-born households).

The Census Bureau estimated from its American Community Survey that in 2002 the foreign-born population of the United States was about 33,048,800 persons. The chart below shows the regions from which those foreign residents came.

United States
Foreign Born by Source

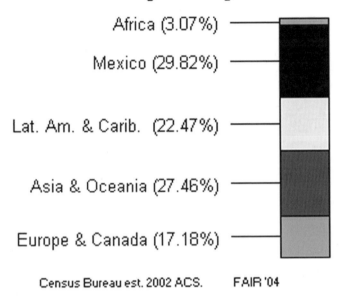

Africa (3.07%)

Mexico (29.82%)

Lat. Am. & Carib. (22.47%)

Asia & Oceania (27.46%)

Europe & Canada (17.18%)

Census Bureau est. 2002 ACS.   FAIR '04

DISTRIBUTION OF THE FOREIGN BORN INCREASE

Eleven states had increases of more than 400,000 foreign-born residents between 1970-2000. Four of them had increases of more than one million residents: California, Florida, New York, and Texas. Besides these four states and the other traditional immigrant-settlement states of New Jersey and Illinois, the other newly emergent immigrant high-impact states were Arizona, Georgia, North Carolina, Virginia and Washington.

Foreign-Born Change 1970-2000

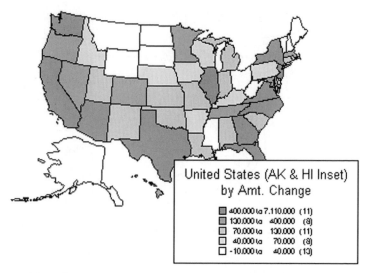

United States (AK & HI Inset)
by Amt. Change

- 400,000 to 7,110,000 (11)
- 130,000 to 400,000 (8)
- 70,000 to 130,000 (11)
- 40,000 to 70,000 (8)
- -10,000 to 40,000 (13)

Twelve states had increases of more than 510 percent in their foreign-born populations between 1970-2000. Three had more than a ten-fold increase: Georgia, Nevada, and North Carolina. Only Texas among traditional immigrant settlement states was included in these top-12 states. The others in this category were Arizona, Arkansas, Colorado, New Mexico, Oklahoma, South Carolina, Tennessee, and Virginia.

Foreign-Born Change 1970-2000

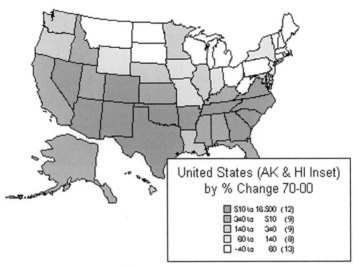

United States (AK & HI Inset)
by % Change 70-00

☐ $10 to 16,500 (12)
☐ 340 to $10 (9)
☐ 140 to 340 (9)
☐ 60 to 140 (8)
☐ -40 to 60 (13)

There were five states that were among those with both the highest rate of change in foreign-born population as well as the highest number of additional foreign-born residents. They were Arizona, Georgia, North Carolina, Texas and Virginia.

THE IMMIGRANT STOCK

According to a 2000 report of the Census Bureau, there were about 55.9 million people in the United States who were "immigrant stock." This is a term that refers to immigrants and their children born here after their arrival. As a national average, that meant that more than one in five U.S. residents (20.4%) was immigrant stock in 2000. The size of the Census Bureau's es-

177

timate of the immigrant stock for each state is shown in the table below. *(http://www.fairus.org/site/PageServer?pagename=research_research9605#table#)*

There are about 10 to 11 million children under the age 18 who are children of immigrants. This information is derived from the Children of Immigrants Longitudinal Study.—the largest research project on the topic in the country. (Source: *The Houston Chronicle,* October 3, 1999)

As the graph below shows, the amount and share of the U.S. population change due to the increase in the foreign stock is rising rapidly. Over the past 34 years, the new immigrants and children born to them have added about 45,857,200 people to the population. Over this period, the increase in the foreign stock has accounted for 50.7 percent of the country's population increase. Since 2000, the increase in the post-1970 foreign stock has been responsible for about 62 percent of the overall population increase.

The increase in the immigrant stock was responsible for all of the population increase since 1970 in Connecticut, Illinois, Massachusetts, New Jersey, New York, Pennsylvania and Rhode Island. It accounted for more than three-quarters of the population increase in California, Iowa, and North Dakota. Three other states had more than half of their population increase since 1970 accounted for by the increase in the immigrant stock: Hawaii, Michigan and Ohio.

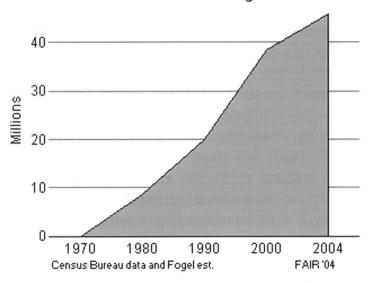

United States
Growth of Post-1970 Foreign Stock

Census Bureau data and Fogel est.   FAIR '04

NET INTERNATIONAL MIGRATION (NIM)

The Census Bureau estimated that in July 2004 the country's population had increased annually by an average of about 3,057,700 residents since 2000 (to 293,655,404 residents). An annual average of about 1,332,410 (or 43.6%) of that increase was directly due to net international migration (more immigrants arriving than leaving) and the remainder was due to a greater number of births than deaths.

For the 1990-99 period, the Census Bureau estimated that the population was growing by about 2,595,990 persons each year. Less than one-third (32%) of that increase (830,900 persons) was estimated to be due to net international migration.

By comparing these two estimates, it can be seen that the current amount of annual population increase is nearly 18 percent higher than during the earlier period. The amount of population change between the two periods attributable to more births than deaths has increased only slightly (about 17,000 per year) while the amount of change attributable to immigration has increased significantly (by more than 528,000 per year).

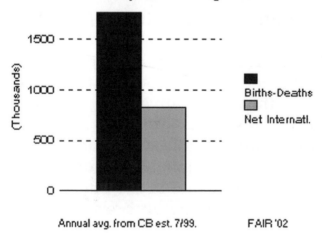

United States
Sources of Population Change 1990-99

Annual avg. from CB est. 7/99.   FAIR '02

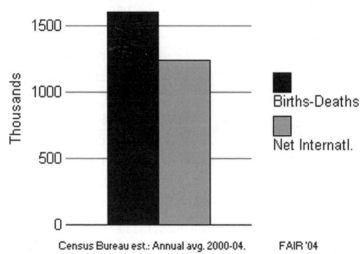

Census Bureau est.: Annual avg. 2000-04. FAIR '04

[Note that these population changes record the children born in United States to immigrants (part of the immigrant stock) as part of the natural change rather than a part of the immigration flow.]

NATURALIZATION

Data from the 2000 Census recorded the U.S. naturalized population at 12,542,626. That was a naturalization rate of 40.3 percent.

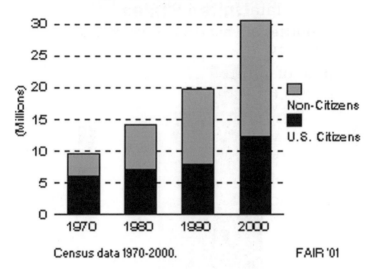

Foreign-Born Population
by Citizenship 1970-2000

Census data 1970-2000.   FAIR '01

Data from the 1990 Census showed that 7,966,998 (40%) of the U.S.'s foreign-born residents (19,767,316) had become naturalized U.S. citizens.

INS DATA ON IMMIGRANT SETTLEMENT

New immigration adds over one-million persons each year when the stream of illegal entrants and visa overstayers is added to legal admissions. The data below describe the legal admissions.

Immigrant settlement in the United States has risen since the adoption of the current immigration system in 1965. The recent rate of new immigrants has about tripled from the rate of the late 1960s. The chart below shows the INS immigrant admissions data since 1965 and the cumulative amount of those immigrant admissions (25,326,749 immigrants as of 2005). The number of annual admissions has ranged from 296,697 in FY'65 to 1,827,167 in FY'91. The higher level of admissions from FY'89-'91 was due the inclusion of illegal immigrants who were given legal status as a result of the Immigration Reform and Control Act (IRCA) amnesty enacted in 1986.

United States
Immigrant Admissions: 1965-2005

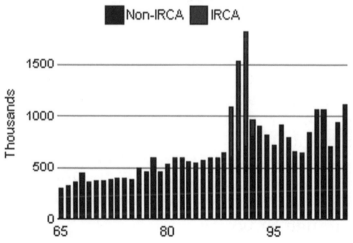

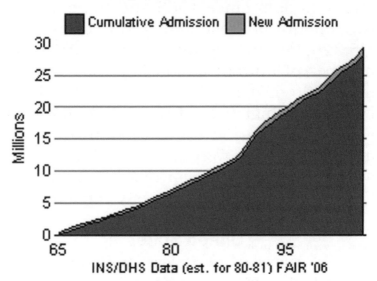

The United States
Immigrant Admissions 1965-05

Each year the government releases annual data on the number of new immigrants. Some are newly arrived from abroad and others may already be in the United States in another status before being granted immigrant status.

Data shows that since 1996 the average number of immigrants admitted for legal residence has been over 835,000 per year (through FY'05).

Countries	96	97	98	99	00	01	02	03	04	05	Total
Bangladesh	8,221	8,678	8,645	6,046	7,215	7,171	5,492	4,616	8,061	11,487	75,632
Canada	15,799	11,595	10,184	8,864	16,210	21,933	19,519	11,350	15,567	21,878	152,899
China*	54,902	53,229	49,135	43,835	60,111	76,918	77,208	51,059	64,068	82,868	613,333
Colombia	14,153	12,945	11,761	9,966	14,498	16,730	18,845	14,720	18,678	25,571	157,867
Cuba	26,209	33,422	17,228	14,132	20,831	27,703	28,272	9,262	20,488	36,261	233,808
D.R.	31,807	22,592	17,391	17,864	17,536	21,313	22,604	26,159	30,492	27,504	235,262
Ecuador	8,305	8,062	6,839	8,904	7,685	9,706	10,602	7,066	8,611	11,608	87,388
El Sal.	17,888	17,958	14,584	14,606	22,578	31,272	31,168	28,231	29,795	21,359	229,439
Germany	6,748	5,619	5,442	5,201	7,638	9,886	8,961	5,064	7,099	9,264	70,922
Guatamala	8,753	7,778	7,752	7,308	9,970	13,567	16,229	14,386	17,999	16,825	120,567
Guyana	9,467	7,228	3,957	3,300	5,746	9,303	9,962	6,809	6,329	9,318	71,419
Haiti	18,368	15,091	13,444	16,532	22,364	27,120	20,268	12,293	13,998	14,529	174,007
Honduras	5,870	7,615	6,445	4,809	5,939	6,615	6,461	4,645	5,505	7,012	60,916
India	44,817	38,048	36,458	30,237	42,046	70,290	71,105	50,228	70,116	84,681	538,026
Iran	11,020	9,646	7,809	7,203	8,519	10,497	13,029	7,230	10,434	13,887	99,274
Ireland	1,731	999	944	812	1,315	1,522	1,425	983	1,531	2,088	13,350
Jamaica	19,073	17,804	15,062	14,733	16,000	15,393	14,898	13,347	14,414	18,346	159,070
Japan	6,011	5,004	5,063	4,217	7,094	9,619	9,301	5,971	7,694	8,768	68,742
Korea	17,991	14,109	13,595	12,840	15,830	20,742	21,021	12,382	19,766	26,561	174,837
Mexico	163,489	146,828	131,534	147,573	173,919	206,426	219,380	115,585	175,364	161,445	1,641,543
Nicaragua	6,903	6,672	3,517	13,389	24,029	19,896	10,850	4,094	4,000	3,305	96,655
Nigeria	10,216	6,699	7,758	6,769	7,853	8,291	8,129	7,872	9,374	10,598	83,559
Pakistan	12,512	12,959	13,093	13,496	14,535	16,448	13,743	9,415	12,086	14,926	133,213
Peru	12,817	10,820	10,137	8,438	9,613	11,131	11,999	9,409	11,781	15,352	111,497
Philippines	53,435	47,235	32,838	31,026	42,474	53,154	51,308	45,250	57,827	60,748	475,295
Poland	15,768	12,038	8,466	8,798	10,114	11,818	12,746	10,510	14,250	15,452	119,960
Sov. U.*	40,737	32,688	30,155	18,985	26,443	56,286	56,936	34,892	42,705	66,007	405,834
T.&T.	7,344	6,362	4,809	4,283	6,660	6,665	5,771	4,138	5,384	6,568	57,984
U.K.	13,584	10,686	8,994	7,690	13,385	18,436	16,181	9,527	14,915	19,800	133,198
Vietnam	42,052	38,494	17,313	20,393	26,747	35,531	33,627	22,087	31,514	32,784	300,542
Yugoslavia*	11,853	10,404	8,007	8,987	17,023	34,620	41,272	8,699	17,024	23,205	181,094
Other	184,998	150,791	119,832	125,332	167,887	178,316	175,420	136,263	179,273	242,368	1,660,480
Total US	902,841	790,098	648,191	646,568	849,807	1,064,318	1,063,732	703,542	946,142	1,122,373	8,737,612

A dash (-) indicates that the data for that year was not published for that country in the Immigration Statistical Yearbook.* China includes Hong Kong and Taiwan. The Soviet Union includes Russia and former parts of the USSR. Yugoslavia includes Bosnia-Herzegovina, Croatia, Macedonia, Montenegro-Serbia, Slovakia and Slovenia.

The data for FY'95, and FY'97-'99 and FY'03 were artificially low because the INS did not issue green cards to all the applicants for adjustment of status who were already in the United States. In those five years, new immigration could have registered as much as 30 percent higher, if the INS had issued more visas. The INS began

185

to catch up with its backlog of adjustment to legal residence in FY'01.

The 31 nationalities above represent more than four-fifths (82%) of all immigrant settlement and adjustment during this ten-year period. Nearly one-fifth (18.8%) of total admissions were accounted for by immigrants from Mexico. With immigrants admitted from China, Philippines, India, the former Soviet Union and Mexico, these constitute more than two-fifths (42%) of all new admissions.

STATE 2000 (in thousands)	Population	Foreign-Born Population	%	Immigrant Stock Population	%	New Immigrants	Illegal Aliens
Alabama	4,447	88	3%	136	3.1%	19	34
Alaska	637	37	5.9%	83	13.3%	13	5
Arizona	5,131	656	13.8%	1,331	35.7%	105	383
Arkansas	2,673	74	3.8%	134	4.6%	15	37
California	33,873	8,864	36.3%	15,896	46.9%	3,163	2,209
Colorado	4,301	370	8.6%	753	17.5%	84	144
Connecticut	3,406	370	10.9%	806	23.7%	101	39
Delaware	784	45	5.7%	71	9.1%	13	10
D.C.	573	74	13.9%	98	17.1%	30	7
Florida	15,983	2,671	16.7%	4,537	29.0%	755	337
Georgia	8,187	577	7.1%	541	6.6%	133	338
Hawaii	1,313	213	17.5%	433	35.7%	67	3
Idaho	1,294	64	5.0%	166	13.8%	18	19
Illinois	12,419	1,539	13.3%	3,477	19.9%	505	432
Indiana	6,081	187	3.1%	370	6.1%	45	45
Iowa	2,936	91	3.1%	375	9.4%	30	34
Kansas	2,688	135	5.0%	308	11.5%	35	47
Kentucky	4,043	80	2.0%	180	4.5%	36	15
Louisiana	4,469	116	3.6%	315	4.8%	33	5
Maine	1,375	37	3.9%	139	10.9%	9	-3
Maryland	5,397	518	9.8%	861	16.3%	183	56
Massachusetts	6,349	773	13.3%	1,708	36.9%	334	87
Michigan	9,938	534	5.3%	1,398	13.1%	161	70
Minnesota	4,930	260	5.3%	500	10.3%	86	60
Mississippi	2,845	40	1.4%	61	3.1%	10	8
Missouri	5,595	151	2.7%	335	6.0%	53	33
Montana	903	16	1.8%	64	7.1%	4	-3
Nebraska	1,711	75	4.4%	156	9.1%	33	34
Nevada	1,998	317	15.8%	576	28.8%	66	101
New	1,336	54	4.4%	174	14.1%	16	-3

REFUGEE SETTLEMENT

The nation has received nearly 630,600 refugees over the most recent eight fiscal years (FY'96-'03) for permanent resettlement. This is an average of nearly 79,000 refugees per year. Refugee admissions have been at a lower level since FY'02 because of heightened security screening procedures and because of concern over fraud in the family reunification eligibility criteria.

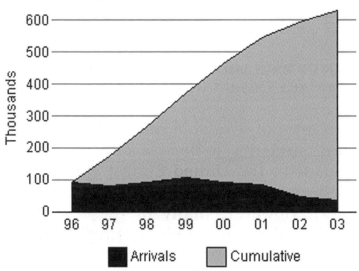

United States
Refugee Settlement FY'96 - FY'03

Under the Office of Refugee Resettlement's (HHS) assistance funding for FY'02, $71,900,000 is available for refugee employment training and other services programs based on a three-year refugee settlement program covering 284,646 refugees. This allocation does not include a larger share (55%) of funding programs for communities heavily affected by recent Cuban and Haitian entrants ($19 million), communities with refugees whose cultural differences make assimilation especially difficult ($26 million), communities impacted by federal welfare reform changes ($14 million), educational support to schools with significant refugee students ($15 million), and discretionary grants ($12.7 million). The FY'02 total of all these programs is $158.6 million (an average of $557 per refugee).

LIMITED ENGLISH PROFICIENCY/ENGLISH LANGUAGE LEARNING STUDENTS

Data are not available nationally on immigrant students (either legally or illegally resident in the United States) who are enrolled in primary and secondary schools (K-12). However, many of these students are enrolled in Limited English Proficiency/English Language Learning (LEP/ELL) instruction programs. Many may be U.S.-born, but nearly all of these students may be assumed to be either immigrants or the children of immigrants, with the exception being in localities that have native American students who speak a language other than English.

K-12 Enrolment - LEP Students
School Years '89-'90 to '99-'00

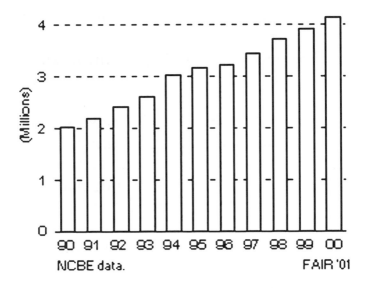

NCBE data.   FAIR '01

LEP data are missing '92-94 for Pa., Va., WV; '95 for Va. WV; '96 for Pa., WV; '97 for Pa., Va., WV; '98 for WV, Col.; '99 for Col.

While K-12 enrollment nationwide has risen by nine percent from the '92-'93 school year to the '91-'92 school year, the enrollment of LEP/ELL students has soared much more rapidly, i.e., by 58.6 percent over the same period. In the '01-'02 school year, LEP/ELL enrollment was about 4,057,000, excluding Puerto Rico and U.S. territories.

Data on enrollment in LEP/ELL programs is collected by the federal government from school systems that receive Title VII funds for these special instruction programs. The data on LEP/ELL enrollment are understated because data on enrollment in private schools that do not apply for Title VII assistance are sketchy. In the '96-'97 school year, 98.9 percent of the reported LEP enrollment was from public schools.

The distribution of LEP enrollment, like the distribution of immigrants, is concentrated in a few states. California accounts for 37 percent of '01-'02 national total. Texas accounts for nearly 15 percent of the total, Florida for 7 percent, New York for nearly 7 percent and Illinois for about 3.5 percent. Those five states together account for more than two-thirds (69%) of all LEP/ELL students in the country. Ten years earlier, however, these same five states accounted for 75 percent of all of the LEP students. This demonstrates the rapid rise in the immigrant population in other areas of the country.

FOREIGN STUDENTS

The 2004/05 annual "Open Doors" report of the Institute of International Education (IEE) shows a 1.3 percent decrease in foreign students attending U.S. colleges and universities from a year earlier. However, international student enrollment has steadily grown as a percentage of overall enrollment in higher education, and this year remained at 4.0 percent very similar to last year. To put this into perspective, until 1979-80 international student enrollment was never higher than 1.7 percent of overall enrollment. Then it jumped in that year to 2.4 percent and then continued to slowly climb until it hit 3.1 percent in 1996-97. Foreign student enrollment then jumped again to 3.6 percent the following year and has continued to climb to its current level. Users of the IIE data should keep in mind that the 565,039 foreign students reported by IIE understates the actual total because of missing data from some schools, and it only includes students on visas and, therefore, does not include foreign students in the country illegally or with other than student visas. The chart below shows the sharp increase in foreign students attending school in the United States from 1960-2000

The countries with the largest numbers of foreign students were India 80,466), China (62,523), Korea (53,358), Japan (42,215), Canada (28,140), and Taiwan (25914,).

The United States
Foreign Students in Post Secondary Education

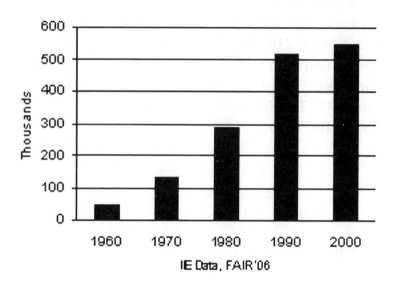

IE Data, FAIR'06

POPULATION PROJECTION

The chart (below) is based on a projection of U.S. population growth through the year 2050. The projection was done by the Census Bureau in 1996 with different assumptions (scenarios). The two scenarios depicted in the chart are for zero-net immigration and the "middle series" based on the current demographic trend, including immigration. FAIR judges that the middle series projection understates future population growth, because the assumptions about the level of both legal and illegal immigration appear to be too low. (This assessment was borne out when the Census Bureau released in 2002 a preliminary projection that recalculated the earlier projection using the higher-than-expected population found in the 2000 Census. The new mid-level population projection for 2025 was 349.7 million residents, and for 2050, it was for 420.1 million residents.)

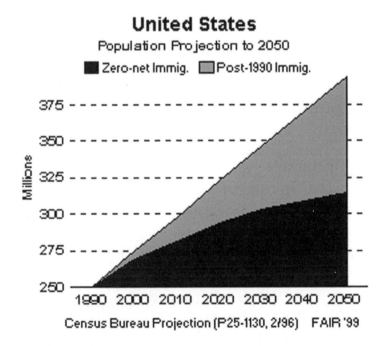

United States

Population Projection to 2050

■ Zero-net Immig. □ Post-1990 Immig.

Census Bureau Projection (P25-1130, 2/96)   FAIR '99

The zero-net scenario assumes the number of new immigrants coming into the country balances those who leave or die. The difference of about 80 million people between the two scenarios depicts the impact of post-1990 immigrants and their offspring on the size of U.S. population. That amount shows how today's and tomorrow's immigrants and their offspring are likely to account for over 60 percent of the nation's population growth over the next half century if nothing is done to change current policies.

In the Census Bureau's "high" immigration projection, assuming annual net immigration of 1,370,000, the population in 2025 is more than six percent higher than in the middle projection, and it is over 11 percent higher by 2050. The high immigration projection would mean a U.S. population in 2050 of 438,299,000 people. If today's mass immigration were significantly scaled back, the population increase attributable to immigration could be significantly reduced over time. The 1997 Census Bureau population projection has the nation growing by 27.5 percent between 1995 and 2025 (increasing more than 60 million above the 1995-estimated population to 335,048,000). However, when the Census Bureau made this estimate, it projected the population in 2000 would be about 275 million, rather than the 281.4 million found by the 2000 Census. When the Census Bureau recalculated the projection in 2002 to account for the additional 6.4 million residents in 2000, it calculated that the population would increase by 68.3 million residents (24.3%) by 2025. And, if the rate of increase between 1990 and 2000 were continued, the population in 2025 would be nearing 400 million, 40.8 percent greater than in 2000—as shown below.

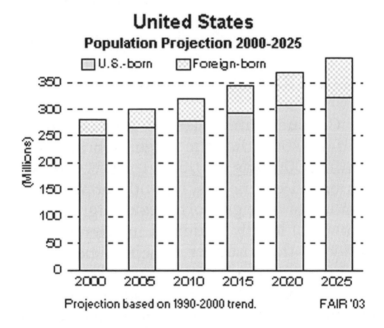

United States
Population Projection 2000-2025

☐ U.S.-born   ☒ Foreign-born

Projection based on 1990-2000 trend.   FAIR '03

The projection above reflects different rates of change for the U.S.-born and foreign-born segments of the population. The U.S.-born population is increasing at slightly less than one percent per year. The foreign-born population is increasing at over 3.8 percent per year. This differential rate is why the foreign-born share increased from less than five percent in 1970 to 11 percent in 2000. Unless there is a change in the immigration law or in its enforcement, a continuation of this trend could result in the foreign-born share of the population over the next 25 years exceeding the highest level ever recorded in the United States—15 percent in 1890—and continuing to rise to 18.6 percent in 2025 and with no end in sight.

ILLEGAL RESIDENT ALIENS

The Census Bureau issued an estimate in January 2002 that the illegal alien population in 2000 was 8,705,421. That estimate was based on the discrepancy between the number of foreign-born residents and the number of legally admitted immigrants. Included in that number may be aliens residing in the United States under provisions that preclude their deportation, but who are not legal permanent residents, such as beneficiaries of Section 245(i) petitions, or asylum-seekers who have not been in the country long enough for adjustment of status, or Central American beneficiaries of the NACARA legislation.

FAIR increased its estimate of the illegal alien population in mid-2004 to 10-12 million persons. The Center for Immigration Studies estimated this population at 10 million as of 2004. A much higher estimate of as many as 20 million illegal aliens by Bear-Stearns analysts in January 2005 was based on trend data in housing starts, school enrollment and remittances as well as a misunderstanding of the methodology used in lower official government estimates. The Bear-Stearns analysts also relied on an estimate by *TIME Magazine* journalists that the annual influx of illegal aliens is about three million persons. This estimate was based on an overestimate of the number of illegal immigrants being apprehended.

The Immigration and Naturalization Service estimated the size of the nation's illegal immigration problem at five million residents (in the country for at least a year) as of 1996. The INS also estimated that the illegal immigrant population was rising a net amount of 275,000 per year, i.e., adding up to about 6.1 million in 2000. And, the Census Bureau estimated the illegal alien population to be increasing by 225,000 per year. In light of the 2000 Census findings, it is clear that the net increase in the illegal alien population has been around 400,000 to 500,000 per year.

The INS issued an estimate in February 2003 that the illegal alien population (in the country for more than one year) in 2000 was seven million and that it grew between 1990-2000 by about 350,000 per year. This annual increase was about 75,000 per year higher than its previous estimate in 1998. The INS estimate does not include certain categories of aliens who entered the country illegally or overstayed their entry permit, such as persons granted Temporary Protected Status and given work permits after a natural disaster or political instability in their home country leads to a decision to halt their deportation.

In the new INS estimate, the share of illegal aliens attributed to entry permit overstays was put at one third, down from 39 percent in the 1998 estimate. That meant that two-thirds of the illegal alien population had sneaked into the country (Entered Without Inspection, or EWI in INS parlance).

In February 2001, researchers at Northeastern Univ. released a finding that the illegal alien population may have grown to as many as 11 million. The research pointed to illegal immigration as the only plausible explanation for the unexpectedly large number of residents in the country found in the 2000 Census and the discrepancy between payroll data and employment data collected by the Bureau of Labor Statistics. Asked by the *Boston Globe* about the finding, Census Director Kenneth Prewitt said "it is clear that the number of undocumented immigrants is higher [than the INS estimate], but how much higher is unknown." (*Boston Globe*, Feb. 6, 2001.

Other estimates by independent researchers include one published in *Demography* in August 2001 that put the total illegal population at 7.1 million (3.9 million Mexicans) and another in the same month by a demographer at the Urban Institute who put the total illegal alien population at 8.5 million (4.5 million Mexicans).

INCARCERATION COSTS OF ILLEGAL IMMIGRANTS

State and local jurisdictions receive partial compensation under the federal State Criminal Alien Assistance Program (SCAAP) established in 1994 to help defray the costs of incarceration of deportable aliens who are serving time for a felony conviction or at least two misdemeanors. Recent budgets submitted by the Bush administration have attempted to end the program by omitting any funding request. Congress, nevertheless, has continued to fund the program.

Recent SCAAP distributions to the states and local jurisdictions have been:

FY'99—$573   million
FY'00—$569   million

FY'01—$535   million
FY'02—$543   million
FY'03—$240   million
FY'04—$282 million
FY'05—$287 million
FY'06—$376 million (available, but not yet distributed)

The SCAAP program covers only a share of corrections staff salaries related to the incarceration of criminal aliens. Other expenses such as the feeding, clothing, and medical attention provided to those prisoners are not included in the compensation calculation. According to House Concurrent Resolution 95, which passed the U.S. Senate on March 26, 2003, the "costs associated with the incarceration of undocumented criminal aliens" cost state and local governments more than $13 billion in FY'02.

The amount of SCAAP awards has leveled off after declining significantly in both total distributions and as a share of the state's expenses, which have been rising. In FY'99, the states and local jurisdictions received less than 39 percent of their itemized salary expenses. SCAAP data from FY'02 indicate that the level of compensation fell to less than 20 percent of expenses. Meanwhile, SCAAP data indicate that the amount of illegal alien detention increased between FY'99 and FY'02 by about 45 percent (from about 25.3 thousand prisoner years to about 36.6 thousand prisoner years), while compensation decreased by five percent, and it dropped precipitously the following year.

Recent SCAAP awards have fluctuated, with the most recent awards in FY'05 representing 33.5 percent of that portion of reported salary costs related to incarceration of criminal aliens. Earlier recent distributions were 42.2 percent in FY'04, and 33.9 percent in FY'03. The Department of Homeland Security, which administers the SCAAP program, has ceased publicly releasing information on the data submissions by the states, but data for FY'04 and FY'03 indicate that the level of prisoner years used in the calculation of SCAAP awards has leveled off: FY'04 74,363, FY'03 74,603.

MEDICAL COSTS OF ILLEGAL ALIENS

Under the Emergency Medical Treatment and Labor Act, hospitals with emergency rooms are required to treat and stabilize patients with emergency medical needs regardless of whether they are in the country legally or whether they are able to pay for the treatment. Congress in 2003 enacted an appropriation of $250 million per year (for 4 years) to help offset some of the costs due to use of this service by illegal aliens. These costs under Medicaid and Medicare were estimated in 1997 by Dr. Huddle of Rice University at $3.2 billion (see *The Cost of Immigration:* http://www.fairus.org/site/PageServer?pagename=iic_immigrationissuecenters87d3). With the size of the illegal alien population more than doubled since that time and the increase in the cost of medical care, the costs today would be much higher.

Appendix G[*]
FAIR Tax[lxxviii]

Introduction

Annexation of Mexico, with all the social and economic changes it would bring makes it a perfect time to discuss another government bureaucracy-fostered bugbear that must be addressed, and it is quite germane to the annexation issue: Our tax code.

Imagine a tax system that:

- Allows you to keep 100% of your pay-check, pension, and Social Security payments.
- Frees up the time wasted on filling out cumbersome I.R.S. forms.
- Makes taxation of income unconstitutional by repealing the 16th Amendment.
- Exempts all taxpayers from federal taxation, up to the poverty level, through a monthly rebate.
- Ensures that all Americans pay their fair share of taxes.

---

[*] Note that the "FAIR Tax is unrelated to the FAIR organization cited in the previous appendix.

- Dramatically lowers tax rates for low-income and middle-income Americans.
- Dramatically reduces the cost of goods and services by 20% to 30%.
- Allows families to save more for home ownership, education, and retirement.
- Protects and ensures the funding of Social Security and Medicare.
- Leaves unchanged the amount of money raised by the federal government.
- Makes American products more competitive overseas.

How? This tax system is the most researched, and we think you'll agree, the best tax reform plan—it's called the Fair-Tax (SM). (http://www.fairtax.net)

The Problem is the Current Income Tax Code

A. The current tax code is unfair, costly, and unreasonably confusing.

- Because the tax code is so complex and easy to evade, many of us pay more in taxes per year than we should! The I.R.S. estimates that over 40% of Americans no longer comply with the current tax code! This makes the rest of us pay over 30% more in taxes.

- Over half of American taxpayers seek professional help simply to prepare their returns. And according to Money Magazine, chances are 99% that you will pay someone to file an incorrect return!

- Compliance with the tax code is not only very difficult and complicated, but unreasonably expensive as well. It is estimated that it costs taxpayers $225 billion for tax filing, tax record keeping, and tax reduction advice. That's the equivalent of about $850 for every man, woman and child in America! We have taxation without comprehension!

B. The current income tax code unfairly hampers personal financial opportunity.

- When citizens are taxed on their earnings and on what they produce, hard work is discouraged.

- The current income tax code inhibits economic growth, capital formation, and, most importantly, job creation.

205

- The current income tax code punishes personal savings and investments; and sometimes these are unfairly subjected to double and even triple taxation.

C. The current income tax code tax is grossly unfair to all wage-earning Americans.

- Payroll taxes are taken out of our paychecks, and we have no control or choice over when we pay or how much we pay in taxes. They are deducted from our paychecks before we can save or spend it.

- The payroll tax is the most regressive and unfair feature of our current tax system. The current payroll tax applies only to wages, and hurts the most important tool by which anyone who is not born to wealth has to get ahead.

D. The current tax system allows for massive loopholes, encouraging politicians and lobbyists to pick winners and losers.

- The tax code is filled with loopholes that are manipulated by high-priced lobbyists for their clients, and by other special interests.

- The complexity of the current income tax code is an open invitation to those with the means to manipulate the tax code.

- There are more lobbyists registered in Washington for taxes than for any other issue.

The Solution is the FairTax

The FairTax is fair to all Americans and simple to understand. Under the FairTax, all wage earners will keep 100% of their paychecks, prices will drop dramatically, and Social Security and Medicare funding will be more secure.

The FairTax frees up financial opportunity by restoring choice in spending, encouraging savings and investment, and dramatically reducing tax evasion. With the elimination of virtually all compliance costs, $225 billion will be restored to the economy. The FairTax offers an unprecedented opportunity for lower and middle-income wage earners to get ahead, to save to buy a house, to educate themselves and their children, and to save for a dignified retirement. And under the FairTax, all

Americans, regardless of their income level, will be better off with the FairTax.

- Everyone will be subject to the same consumption tax rate with no exceptions and no exclusions, and those least able to share in the cost of government will carry no federal tax burden at all.

- The FairTax increases individual purchasing power, making it easier to get ahead financially by eliminating:

    - the individual income tax, including capital gains taxes

    - the payroll income tax

    - the inheritance tax and the gift tax

    - the self-employment tax

    - the corporate income tax

The solution we propose involves two actions:

- Passage of legislation that institutes a single-rate, FairTax on all final sales of new goods and services. This tax would become the chief source of revenue for the United States government, replacing all federal income and payroll taxes, yet generating the same revenue. The legislation provides for a tax rebate equal to the consumption tax paid on essential goods and services. The rebate ensures that no American will pay tax on the purchase of necessities.

- A constitutional amendment that would repeal the 16th Amendment and make a federal income tax unconstitutional.

We Can Win!

Bringing the FairTax to a vote only requires 31 members of Congress! If eleven members of the Senate Finance Committee and twenty members of the Ways and Means Committee support the FairTax, they can bring the FairTax Bill out of their respective committees and onto the floor of both the House and the Senate. At that point, it would be the leadership's decision to go to a full vote by the entire membership. It can be done, and we are well on our way there. Polling shows that the American people understand and favor fundamental reform such as a federal consumption tax. The national groundswell of support is growing in leaps and bounds. Thousands of Americans are expressing their support for the FairTax through phone calls, e-mails, letters, and faxes. FairTax Volunteers are growing by the hundreds. The possibility of bringing about peaceful change is one of the great strengths of the American system. It is obvious that the FairTax is a reasonable solution whose time has come.

Let me repeat the tremendous benefits of the FairTax plan. The FairTax plan:

- Allows you to keep 100% of your paycheck, pension, and Social Security payments.

- Frees up the time wasted on filling out cumbersome I.R.S. forms.
- Makes taxation of income unconstitutional by repealing the 16th Amendment.

- Exempts all taxpayers from federal taxation, up to the poverty level, through a monthly rebate.

- Ensures that all Americans pay their fair share of taxes.

- Dramatically lowers tax rates for low-income and middle-income Americans.

- Dramatically reduces the cost of goods and services by 20% to 30%.

- Allows families to save more for home ownership, education, and retirement.

- Protects and ensures the funding of Social Security and Medicare.

- Leaves unchanged the amount of money raised by the federal government.

- Makes American products more competitive overseas.

As Americans come to understand that the FairTax will close tax loopholes and make everyone pay their fair share of taxes, it will be passed into law. Fully 85% of Americans informed about the FairTax are likely to support the tax change that makes the closing of these loopholes a reality. And the FairTax offers not only this, but many other benefits:

- You never pay another hidden tax again. The FairTax is printed on every receipt for every purchase.

- All taxpayers are treated fairly. No loopholes for anyone.

- Individuals have more control and choice. People can make choices about how much to pay in taxes, by deciding when to buy and what to buy.

- Virtually all economic models project a much healthier economy under the FairTax. Real investment will grow by an estimated 76.4 percent. Exports will jump by an estimated 26.4 percent. Interest rates will drop between 20 and 30 percent.

- Small businesses never have to track tax withholdings or deductions.

- Tax evasion will dramatically decrease. No more income reporting means the end of "hiding" income from tax authorities.

- Compliance costs will be slashed. Compliance costs will drop by over 90%, from $225 billion.

Concluding Remarks

It is time for the FairTax. For nearly 100 years, we have carried the burden of an oppressive and counterproductive tax system which has punished work and achievement, savings, and investment. The current tax code has been grossly manipulated to reward elite political interests, and it hurts the average American. The current tax code has hidden the true cost of government from the very taxpayers who pay for it.

Americans are not obligated to accept a tax system that penalizes the average working American while giving special consideration to those who buy favors and perks in Washington, D.C. To be competitive in the next century, and to renew the American dream, we must change the way we fund our national government. It is time for the FairTax.

The FairTax will allow Americans to keep 100% of their paychecks, dramatically reduce prices, protect and ensure funding of Social Security and Medicare, empower low-income taxpayers, and put choice and control back into the hands of all Americans. All the crucial elements are in place: a public, eager and ready for a tax system that is fair, and a Congress seriously willing to consider genuine tax reform. It only takes thirty-one Congressmen, and we will win.

Appendix H
References

Abbot, Gorham, *Mexico and the United States: Their Mutual Relations and Common Interests,* G.P. Putnam and Son, 1869

Andreas, Peter and Biersteker, Thomas, *The Rebordering of North America: Integration and Exclusion in a New Security Context,* Routeledge, 2003.

Andreas, Peter, *Border Games: Policing the US-Mexico Divide,* Cornell University Press, 2000.

Buchanan, Patrick J., *State of Emergency: The Third World Invasion and Conquest of America,* Thomas Dunne Books, 2006.

Clement, Norris, et al, *North American Economic Integration: Theory and Practice,* Edward Elgar Publishing Ltd, 1999.

Foster, John and McChesney, Robert (ed.), *Pox Americana: Exposing the American Empire,* Monthly Review Press, 2004.

Foster, John, *Naked Imperialism: The US Pursuit of Global Dominance,* Monthly Review Press, 2006.

Gilchrist, Jim and Corsi, Jerome, *Minutemen, The Battle to Secure America's Borders,* World Ahead Publishing, 2006.

Hakim, Peter and Litan, Robert, *The Future of North American Integration: Beyond NAFTA,* Brookings Institute Press, 2002.

Kinzer, Stephen, *Overthrow: America's Century of Regime Change from Hawaii to Iraq,* Times Books, 2006.

Lorey, David, *The US-Mexican Border in the Twentieth Century,* SR Books, 1999.

Nevins, Joseph, *Operation Gatekeeper: The Rise of the "Illegal Alien" and the Making of the US-Mexico Boundary*, Routledge, 2002.

Pastor, Robert A., *Toward a North American Community: Lessons from the Old World for the New*, Institute for International Economics, 2001.

Tancredo, Tom, *In Mortal Danger: The Battle for America's Border and Security*, WND Books, 2006.

Weinberger, Casper and Schweizer, Peter, *The Next War*, Regnery Publishing, Inc., 1996.

Wooldridge, Frosty, *Immigration's Unarmed Invasion: Deadly Consequences*, Author House, 2004.

216

Appendix I
Endnotes

[i] Walker, Francis A., *The Atlantic Monthly*, June, 1896; vol. 77, no. 464, pages 822-829

[ii] Gutiérrez, Marcos, *La Oferta Review*, San Jose, CA August 25, 1993

[iii] Mahathir bin Mohamad, Dr. Dato Seri, Prime Minister of Malaysia, in a speech delivered at the First Southern Africa International Dialogue at Kasane, Botswana, May 5, 1997.

[iv] Bartlett and Steele, "Who Left the Door Open?" *Time Magazine*, September 20, 2004.

[v] International Monetary Fund national statistics on employment from http://imfStatistics.org

[vi] Kennedy, John F., *A Nation of Immigrants*, Harper and Row, 1965, pp. 17, 51, 58.

[vii] Dougherty, Jon E, "Anchors Away," *Voices*, May 10, 2005

[viii] See www.cis.org.

[ix] See http://www.cms.hhs.gov/EMTALA

[x] Coronado, Roberto and Gilmer, Robert, "US Mexico Deepen Economic Ties," Federal Reserve Bank of Dallas, Issue 1, Jan/Feb 2006.

[xi] See www.amren.com/mexguide/mexguide.html

[xii] Tancredo, Tom, *In Mortal Danger*, WND Books, 2006, page 147

[xiii] Weinberger, Casper and Schweizer, Peter, *The Next War*, Regenery Publishing, Inc., 1996, page 143

[xiv] See http://www.carryingcapacity.org/huddlenr.html

[xv] See www.fairus.org

[xvi] See www.carryingcapacity.org

[xvii] See www.stoptheinvasion.com

[xviii] See http://ksghome.harvard.edu/~GBorjas/WSJ042696.htm

[xix] Stewart, David W., *Immigration and Education: The Crisis and the Opportunites*, 1993.

[xx] See also www.mnforsustain.org

[xxi] Camarota, Steven A. "Immigrants at Mid-Decade: A Snapshot of America's Foreign-Born Population in 2005," *Backgrounder*, Center for Immigration Studies (December, 2005), pp. 2.

[xxii] Rubenstein, Edwin S., "The Stupid Americans? Look Again," VDARE.com, December 22, 2005

[xxiii] See "Student who sat for Mexican anthem rebuked," www.worldnetdaily.com, October 7, 2005.

[xxiv] *Los Angeles Times*, March 23, 1993.

[xxv] Macdonald, Heather, "the Illegal Alien Crime Wave," *City Journal*, Winter, 2004.

[xxvi] Arizona Department of Motor Vehicles statistic

[xxvii] "President Discusses Border Security and Immigration Reform in America," www.whitehouse.gov/news/releases/2005/11, Nov. 28, 2005

[xxviii] "Criminal Aliens" on www.fairus.org

[xxix] Dougherty, Jon E., "Illegal Immigration's Financial Impact," *Freedom Alliance Policy Paper* on www.freedomalliance.org

[xxx] Office of Management and Budget, Executive Office of the President, *the Budget of the United States Government, Fiscal Year 2006*, GPO, 2006.

[xxxi] Seper, Jerry, "Illegal Criminal Aliens Abound in US," *Washington Times*, January 26, 2004.

[xxxii] Wahla, Lisa, "Illegal Aliens Drain County Funds," *Antelope Valley Press,* December 26, 2000.

[xxxiii] See www.vdare.com, September 30, 2004

[xxxiv] US Center for Disease Control and Prevention

[xxxv] Patterson, Kevin, "Patient Predator," *Mother Jones News,* March, 2003

[xxxvi] Cosman, Madeleine Pelner, "The Seen and Unseen," *Journal of American Physicians and Surgeons* 10, no. 1, Spring 2005

[xxxvii] Rockefeller, John D. III, "Report of the Commission on Population Growth and the American Future," March 27, 1972

[xxxviii] Nelson, Gaylord, Conference on Immigration, November 5, 1993

[xxxix] Nelson, Gaylord, *Newhouse News Service*, May 21, 2001.

[xl] "US Border Patrol Facing new Illegal Immigration Problems," *Voices,* June 30, 2005

[xli] Wooldridge, Frosty, *Immigration's Unarmed Invasion: Deadly Consequences*, Author House, 2004, page 14

[xlii] "President Discusses Border Security and Immigration Reform in America," Tucson, Arizona, Office of the Press Secretary, The White House, Nov. 28, 2005

[xliii] "Dearborn Man Pleads Guilty to Conspiracy to Provide Support to Hezbollah," Press Release, US Attorney, Eastern District of Michigan, Department of Justice, March 1, 2005

[xliv] "FBI Mueller: Hezbollah Busted in Mexican Smuggling Operation," *NewsMax.com*, March 30, 2006.

[xlv] Tancredo, Tom, *In Mortal Danger*, WND Books, 2006, page 86

[xlvi] ibid, page 80

[xlvii] Andreas, Peter, *Border Games: Policing the US Mexico Divide*, Cornell University Press, 2000, Page 90.

[xlviii] Cornelius, Wayne, "The Structural Embeddedness of Demand for Mexican Immigrant Labor: New Evidence from California," in Marcelo Suarez-Orozco (ed.), *Crossings: Mexican Immigration in Interdisciplinary Perspectives*, Harvard University Press, pp. 115-144.

xlix Weinberger, Casper and Schweizer, Peter, *The Next War*, Regnery Publishing, Inc., 1996.

l Kaplan, Robert d. 1998, *An Empire Wilderness: Travels into America's Future.* New York: Random House, quoted in Custred, Glynn, "North American Borders: Why They matter", April 2003

li Foster, John, *Naked Imperialism: The US Pursuit of Global Dominance*, Monthly Review Press, 2006, *page 69*

lii Kinzer, Stephen, *Overthrow: America's Century of Regime Change from Hawaii to Iraq*, Times Books, 2006.

liii Lorey, David, *The US-Mexican Border in the Twentieth Century*, SR Books, 1999, pages 129 and 159

liv Kaplan, 1998, quoted in Glynn Custred "North American Borders: Why they Matter", April 2003

lv Carpenter, "Mexico, the Next Colombia" as quoted in Gilchrist, *Minutemen*, Page 171

lvi ibid.

lvii ibid, page 152

lviii White, Deborah, "Illegal Immigration Explained—Profits and Poverty, Social Security and Starvation," *About.com*

lix "2006 Index of Economic Freedom," The Heritage Foundation, www.heritage.org

lx Pastor, *Toward a North American Community*

lxi ibid, page 35

lxii Hakim, T*he Future of North American Integration: Beyond NAFTA, page 4*

lxiii San Diego Union Tribune, October 3, 2002.

lxiv Showley, "A Tale of Two Cities Slowly, Inexorably, Inextricably Linked", *The San Diego Union Tribune*, November 3, 1991.

lxv Pastor, Robert A., *Toward a North American Community: Lessons from the Old World for the New*, Institute for International Economics, 2001, page 69

lxvi ibid, *page 162-163*

lxvii ibid, page 156

lxviii Appiah, Anthony, "The Multiculturalist Misunderstanding," *New York Review of Books*, October 9, 1997.

lxix Hakim, Peter and Litan, Robert, *The Future of North American Integration: Beyond NAFTA*, Brookings Institute Press, 2002, page 24

lxx http://home.att.net/~mwhodges/education-a.htm

lxxi http://en.wikipedia.org/wiki/Education_in_Mexico

lxxii http://www.germanculture.com.ua/library/facts/bl_reunification_afterm ath.htm

219

lxxiii
http://www.customs.gov/xp/cgov/newsroom/fact_sheets/border/secure_
border_initiative/secure_border.xml

lxxiv http://www.cbp.gov/xp/cgov/toolbox/about/history/ins_history.xml

lxxv See
http://www.cbp.gov/xp/cgov/border_security/antiterror_initiatives/safe
guarding_america.xml

lxxvi http://www.amren.com/mexguide/mexguide.html

lxxvii
http://www.fairus.org/site/PageServer?pagename=research_research96
05 (used with kind permission of Jack Martin, FAIR Special Projects
Director.)

lxxviii http://fairtaxvolunteer.org/materials/talking_points.html